Praise for
The Three Success Secrets of Shamgar . . .

"This well-written publication is filled with inspirational stories and truths reassuring us that it is never too late to reach our goals or to make a difference. This interesting text will motivate you to seize every opportunity and to work with your resources at hand to deal with the things that really matter."

—J.B. Hunt
founder and senior chairman
J.B. Hunt Transport Services, Inc.

"*The Three Success Secrets of Shamgar* will prove to be a classic. Although the three principles are simple, the book is anything but simplistic. Applying these principles will prove to be a transforming experience in your life."

—Dwight "Ike" Reighard
Chief People Officer, HomeBanc Mortgage Corporation

"Jay Strack and Pat Williams are two of the most inspirational people I know. They have hit their highest level with this new book on Shamgar. It's going to become an inspirational classic."

—Dave Wannstedt
head coach, Miami Dolphins

"*The Three Success Secrets of Shamgar* will inspire anyone at any age. In a day when the world is in such tension and turmoil, there is hope for the readers that they may make a difference—starting where they are, using what they have and doing what they can. This book will give hope and inspire any reader at any age to believe they can take action to make a difference in the impossible odds most of us face in our society today."

—Vonette Z. Bright
co-founder, Campus Crusade for Christ
founder, National Prayer Committee
founder, Women Today International

The Three Success Secrets of Shamgar

Lessons from an Ancient Hero of Faith and Action

Pat Williams and Jay Strack

with Jim Denney

Health Communications, Inc.
Deerfield Beach, Florida

www.hci-online.com

**Library of Congress Cataloging-in-Publication Data
is available from the Library of Congress.**

Faith Communications (FC), its Logos and Marks are trademarks of Health Communications, Inc.

Publisher: Faith Communications, Inc.
An Imprint of Health Communications, Inc.
3201 S.W. 15th Street
Deerfield Beach, FL 33442-8190

Cover design by Larissa Hise Henoch
Inside book design by Dawn Von Strolley Grove

This book is dedicated

to Jim Henry,

Senior Pastor at

First Baptist Church of Orlando,

a man who lives the Shamgar secrets

every day of his life.

—P.W.

This book is dedicated with humble gratitude to the

faithful board of directors and their wives

of Student Leadership University

who continue to partner with me

through thirty years of ministry to help students

overcome six-hundred-to-one odds:

Anthony and Vicki Barber

Teed and Linda Boyd

Don and Nancy Bush

Jerry and Bonita Brock

James and Denise Clark

James and Angela Clemmons

Jim and Barbara Fuller

Lockwood and Patricia Holmes

David and Cindy Lassiter

Rick and Karen McKinley

John and Gail Otis

Edwin and Judy Robertson

Sandy and Peggy Sansing

Joey and Lisa Smith

Gary and Susan Strack

Howard and Jan White

Skip and Melinda Wren

—J.S.

Contents

Introduction

One of the great themes of the Bible is, "With God, all things are possible" (Matt. 19:26). We have chosen to *illustrate* this truth by telling the story of an obscure biblical figure named Shamgar. We know very little about this man, but we have drawn some reasonable inferences about his life. For example, we are not directly told that Shamgar was a farmer, but we've inferred as much because the instrument he used—an ox-goad—was a farm implement.

The reader should understand, however, that we are not basing any claims of biblical doctrine or theology on these inferences. The details of Shamgar's story are obscure, and we should always remember to interpret what is cloudy in light of what is clear. The story of Shamgar, as we have interpreted it, is intended only to illustrate truths that are much more clearly stated elsewhere in the Bible.

We hope that this book will inspire you with the belief that God uses ordinary people like you to accomplish extraordinary things, regardless of the odds and the opposition you face. That is the message of *The Three Success Secrets of Shamgar.*

—Pat Williams and Jay Strack

Six Hundred to One

by Pat Williams

The story of the great Hebrew lawgiver and liberator, Moses, fills 136 chapters of the Bible. The story of Joseph, a model of absolute integrity, occupies 21 chapters of the Bible. The life of Jesus—the greatest leader, teacher and prophet in history—is recorded in the first 89 chapters of the New Testament.

So how much space does the Bible devote to this hero named Shamgar? Answer: *Two verses.* That's right, just two verses—a mere forty-two words. Clearly, Shamgar could have used a better press agent.

You're probably wondering, "How important could Shamgar be if that's all the mention he gets in the Bible? What can I learn from a guy whose entire biography consists of forty-two words?"

Read on, my friend, and you'll be amazed at what Shamgar can teach you about successful, effective, influential living. God never wastes his words. Everything he tells us in the Bible is meant to impact our lives. Through those two little verses, God tells us that there is literally *no limit* to what we can achieve if we will learn the lessons of Shamgar's life. We find his story in the Old Testament book of Judges:

*After Ehud came Shamgar son of Anath, who struck down six hun-
dred Philistines with an ox-goad. He too saved Israel.* Judges 3:31

*In the days of Shamgar son of Anath, in the days of Jael, the roads
were abandoned; travelers took to winding paths.* Judges 5:6

What do these two verses tell us?

First, because these verses are found in the book of Judges, we know
that Shamgar lived more than 3,000 years ago in the land of Canaan
(which is today called Palestine, comprising of the nation of Israel and
parts of neighboring countries). The land of Canaan was divided
among dozens of walled city-states that were continually at war against
each other. Shamgar's people were the Hebrews who had migrated into
Canaan after generations of bondage under the pharaohs in Egypt. By
the time Shamgar was born, the great Hebrew leaders, Moses and
Joshua, were long dead. The Hebrews had no king, no leadership.

Second, we know that Shamgar lived in evil, dangerous times. "In
the days of Shamgar," we are told, "the roads were abandoned; travelers
took to winding paths." After the death of Joshua, Israel's great military
leader, the land of Israel was repeatedly overrun by foreign invaders.
The people of Israel avoided the main highways for fear of the bandits
and terrorists, such as the Philistines, who were the Al Qaeda of their
day. With no central government or standing army, Israel was vulner-
able on every side. Those were lawless times, and the Hebrew people
were leaderless and defenseless.

Third, we know that Shamgar was a farmer. How do we know that?
Because he "struck down six hundred Philistines with an ox-goad." An
ox-goad is a long wooden pole that has been tipped with a sharpened
iron point at one end and capped with a flattened chisel-like iron blade
at the other end. Shamgar probably owned two oxen that he used to

pull a plow. The sharp end of the ox-goad was used to poke the tough hide of the oxen to keep them motivated for pulling that plow. The chisel-blade end was used to scrape the plowshare free of roots, thorns and accumulated clay. The ox-goad tells us that Shamgar was a man who spent much of his life in a field, pushing a plow behind a pair of oxen, planting and tending his crops.

Fourth, we know that Shamgar demonstrated more military savvy than Gen. George S. Patton, Gen. "Stormin'" Norman Schwarzkopf, and Gen. Tommy Franks combined! All by himself, he killed six hundred Philistines.

Who were the Philistines? They were a barbarous, violent race of people who occupied the southern coastal area of Palestine, which is now known as the Gaza Strip. The region of Philistia was organized around an alliance of five Philistine cities—Ashkelon, Ashdod, Gath, Gaza and Ekron. The antagonism between Israel and the Philistines began at around the time of Shamgar and continued for centuries to the time of King David and beyond.

When the Romans subjugated the land of Israel, they named it "Palaistina" (the Latin form of the word "Philistia"), deliberately insulting the Jewish people by naming their homeland after their worst enemies. Today, the Palestinian Arabs claim to be descended from the Philistines. However, the Philistines originally came to the Gaza region from the Aegean Islands, not Arabia, so this claim has no historical basis.

Before Shamgar defeated the Philistines and saved Israel, no one would have picked him as a man destined for greatness. He was an ox rancher, a clod-kicker, a man with dirt under his fingernails and ox manure on the soles of his sandals. No one would have looked at him and said, "There's the man who's going to save our nation." Yet this

er single-handedly wiped out six hundred Philistine
ved a nation.

How did he do it?

A Leap of Faith

Shamgar was just an average person—no different from Pat Williams or Jay Strack or you. He was an ordinary flesh-and-blood human being who lived in extraordinary times, just as we do today. He set out to defend his neighbors and his nation from a horde of bloodthirsty invaders, and he succeeded—against six-hundred-to-one odds.

Fact is, if you aren't willing to take on six-hundred-to-one odds, you'll never achieve anything great. Nothing worth doing is ever easy. Significant achievements always involve a high degree of courage, focus, perseverance, and yes, risk.

Every significant accomplishment in human history has been a big risk, a long shot: The Pilgrims' founding of the Plymouth colony in 1620. American independence in 1776. The landing at Normandy on D-Day. The writing of great novels, such as *Gone with the Wind* or *The Lord of the Rings*. The first moon landing. The space shuttle. The founding of Jay Strack's Student Leadership University—or the founding of the Orlando Magic.

In fact, let me tell you how the Magic got started. In 1989, I left a rewarding job as general manager of the Philadelphia 76ers and moved my family to Orlando, Florida, to help build a brand-new NBA basketball team from scratch. It was not a good time for me to leave a secure job in Philly and plunge into such a risky venture. At the time, I had a family of six to feed and for all I knew, I was walking off a financial cliff—and taking my wife and kids with me. I had to take a leap of faith, with no guarantee that there was a safety net at the bottom.

The odds were overwhelmingly against all of us who were working on this dream. The NBA had not promised to award a franchise to Orlando, and we were competing against some much more populous markets, such as Miami, Toronto and Minnesota. Orlando had no arena and no history of pro sports. We were definitely the underdogs.

I had to go out to the community and sell season tickets for a team that didn't exist—and in all probability, never would. I was so driven to turn that dream into a reality that I was selling season tickets anywhere and everywhere I could—even in the checkout line at the health food store!

I had to sell the idea of an Orlando sports franchise to civic leaders and business leaders—and there again, the odds were against us. One challenge that faced us was the construction of the arena. The NBA would not even consider a city without an arena—yet the Orlando city fathers didn't want to invest millions in the construction of an arena without a commitment from the NBA. It was a catch-22 situation.

The key to getting our arena turned out to be an amazing coincidence. I was in Houston to speak at a dinner. In the course of the evening, I bumped into the manager of a Houston television station, Vince Barresi, an old friend from Philadelphia. He casually mentioned that his mother-in-law, Pat Schwartz, was a member of the Orlando city council. He had said the magic word!

I asked Vince to put in a good word with his mother-in-law for our arena, so he called Pat Schwartz, told her how important pro basketball was to the city of Houston—and she ended up being the swing vote in a narrow 3–2 decision in favor of the arena. She had been undecided before talking to Vince. If I hadn't gone to Houston to give that speech, the Orlando Magic probably wouldn't exist today.

Some people would chalk it up to chance and coincidence. But I have found that when you trust God and ask for his help in doing something that is seemingly impossible, "coincidences" tend to multiply and swing the odds in your favor. Why? Because there are no coincidences. There's no such thing as luck. There is only the grace of God and answered prayer.

While we were building this dream called the Orlando Magic, we faced a long chain of seemingly insurmountable hurdles. (For example, there was the day we learned that the franchise fee had jumped from $20 million paid in installments to $32.5 million paid up front!) If just one—*just one!*—of the links in that chain had broken, the whole venture would have collapsed like a house of cards.

Looking back, I realize that leaving Philadelphia and moving to Orlando was a foolish decision. The odds were six hundred to one against us. Yet we persevered and the Orlando Magic played its first regular season game in 1989, and I served as the team's first president and general manager.

There is no question in my mind that the Magic exists in large part because my colleagues and I were operating by the three success secrets of Shamgar. Perhaps building an NBA franchise is not as big an accomplishment as, say, wiping out six hundred Philistines with an ox-goad and saving an entire nation, but I think we did all right. And our accomplishment illustrates what ordinary people can do when they follow the pattern that was laid down by this man from ancient Israel.

How to Beat the Odds

So what are you trying to accomplish? What is your dream, your grand goal in life? Whatever that dream may be, you *can* achieve it, even if the odds are six hundred to one against it. Like Shamgar, you *can* beat the odds, you *can* overcome the obstacles, and you can win.

Look, I know what you're up against, because I've been there. You're facing a challenge that seems too big for you. People are telling you to give up on your goals, to let go of your dreams, to "face reality." You're beginning to think that maybe they're right, maybe you should give up and find something safer to do—something less risky.

Don't even think of quitting, my friend! Don't you dare give up—at least not until you've finished this book!

What do you want to accomplish? What is your impossible dream?

Do you aspire to write the Great American Novel? Start your own business? Rescue homeless children from the streets of Calcutta or Buenos Aires or inner-city Los Angeles? Run for public office? Find a cure for cancer, AIDS or Alzheimer's disease? Be the first man or woman on Mars?

You realize, of course, that the odds are against you—a six-hundred-to-one shot, at least. But so what? Other people, just like you, have beaten those odds and have achieved great things. They have hammered dreams into reality. Shamgar did it. Why shouldn't you?

So what if the whole world bets against you? What does it matter that your family and friends say you don't stand a chance? By the time you finish this book, you'll know something they don't. You'll know the three success secrets of Shamgar. You'll know how to beat those six-hundred-to-one odds—and *win*.

I first heard about the three success secrets of Shamgar from my friend Jay Strack—speaker, author and founder of Student Leadership University. Those three life principles completely transformed the way I look at my personal life, my professional life, my relationship with God and the dreams and goals I pursue every day.

By the time you finish this book, you will have Shamgar's three success principles planted in your heart and soul. They will enlarge your vision, rev up your imagination and propel you toward your dreams.

Now, let me turn the next few pages over to Jay. He'll explain the three success secrets of Shamgar and show you how these three simple life principles can transform your life!

2

Three Simple Secrets

by Jay Strack

In 1984, I was on the platform of the Coliseum in Midland, Texas. Just moments before I was to get up and speak, a man hurried up and handed me a message. It read, "Jay, call your mother's doctor in the hsopital in Orlando." My mother was in the hospital battling cancer, so I had been expecting this message for some time.

I folded the note and made the shortest presentation in history. Immediately afterward, I made arrangements to fly to Orlando by private plane—there was no time to wait for a scheduled airline.

I arrived at the hospital early the next morning, weary from missing a night's sleep. I spent time with Mom, and I conferred with the doctors and my half-brother, Rocky. While I was in the hospital, I kept hearing a page over the intercom: "Mr. Strack, report to the front desk. Mr. Strack, report to the front desk." I knew they couldn't be paging me, because hardly anyone knew I was there. They had to be calling a different Mr. Strack.

But after I had heard the page a number of times, I decided I ought to at least check and make sure it wasn't for me. I went to the front desk and said, "My name is Jay Strack. Have you been paging me?"

The receptionist said, "No, we want *the* Mr. Strack."

Just then, a man approached the desk. He said, "Did I hear you say that your name is Jay Strack?"

"That's right," I said.

"My name is Gary Strack," he said. "I'm the CEO of this hospital— and I'm your brother."

Well, that was a startling introduction! I knew only one brother— my half-brother Rocky, who had the same mother as me, but a different father and a different last name. At the moment, I was dog-tired and stressed out, and I was in no mood for jokes—and I told him so.

"It's no joke," Gary Strack said. "You and I are brothers—well, half-brothers. We have the same dad, but different mothers. My dad was married to my mom before he married your mom. By the way, how is Billie doing?" Billie was my mother's name.

"Well, at the moment," I told him, "my mother is here in your hospital, dying of cancer."

He looked stunned. "Oh," he said, "I'm so sorry to hear that."

A short time later, I lost my mother—but amazingly, I had gained a brother I never knew I had.

Gary and I went on to become fast friends. It turned out that we had a lot of things in common, including very similar type-A personalities. We had also struggled with many of the same issues, including having battled alcohol problems. Gary was highly respected in Orlando and had become CEO of one of the largest health care systems in Florida. Today, Gary and I are more than merely brothers—we are brothers in the Christian faith, and he serves on my board of directors.

Looking back, I remembered getting a message from someone who claimed to be my brother, but I had ignored it, thinking it was a hoax. I asked Gary about that message, and he said that, yes, several years earlier, he had seen me on a TV talk show and had called my home and left a message for me. When he didn't hear back he just let it go until he happened to bump into me at the hospital.

I kid Gary about our dad. "Dad loved you best," I say. "He walked out on each of us when we were six years old—but he stayed six days longer with you than he stayed with me!"

Why am I telling you this story?

As I was reading what Pat said in the previous chapter, I was reminded of the fact that we all face six-hundred-to-one odds in some area of our lives. In my case, the long odds I had to overcome had to do with how crazy and mixed-up my family was. It was six hundred to one that I would ever amount to anything, that I would ever achieve anything in life but my own destruction.

You might be wondering how a man can grow to adulthood completely unaware of the existence of an older brother. Well, to understand how something like that was possible, you'd have to know my family background. Let me introduce you.

"Get on Your Knees and Beg Me"

I was born in Orlando, Florida. My father, a successful businessman, was listed in *Who's Who*, but he was so seldom home that we all said, "Who's he?" He was chairman of the board everywhere but in our home. Others saw my father as a success, but at home we saw another person when the drinking took over his life. He would shout, threaten and beat my mother, and the police would come to our house to break it up.

When I was six years old, my father walked out on my mother, my half-brother, Rocky, and me so that he could be with another woman.

Night after night, I prayed that God would send my daddy home, but it didn't happen. The message I got from my dad's abandonment was: "Jay, you're a loser. You're nobody. You're not important to me, and I don't want you in my life."

After my dad left, my mother worked two or three jobs, trying to hold together what was left of our family. Finally, Mom sat my brother and me down for a tearful announcement: "I can't take care of you both." A few days later, she sent my older brother away to be raised by his grandparents in a more stable environment. I was alone.

My mom dated a lot of guys and went through several marriages. Every man she was attracted to was someone she had met in a bar— in other words, a guy with an alcohol problem. She had already been abandoned by an alcoholic husband, yet she kept going back to guys who were just like him or worse.

With each new man who came into my mom's life, my hopes rose. But inevitably, each "step-dad" who came into our lives would turn out to be a guy who drank—and who hurt us. On more than one occasion, I had to get out my Louisville Slugger baseball bat and tell some guy to quit hitting my mother—or to quit hitting me. The morning after a new "step-dad's" drunken tirades, I'd go to school and all my friends would know about the big fight at our house. I tried to laugh it off around my friends, but inside I was dying.

I got used to the men moving in and out of our house until the summer that one of the men brought his older son. That was the summer I learned about sexual abuse. I wrote dozens of letters to my real dad, begging him to come and rescue me. He never came. He never even answered my letters. Years later, when I was an adult, I had a long talk with my dad. I asked him why he never answered my letters. He said he never received any of them. Then I knew: Mom had never mailed them.

At the time, when my letters went unanswered, I suspected she had stopped them—but I refused to believe it.

After six or so men moved in and out, one moved in who promised to stay. He actually married my mom. "Jay," he said, "you can call me Dad, and I will treat you like my own son." I was so excited to have a dad again that I went to school the next day and told all my friends about him. I really bragged him up. I even told my friends that he played third base for the Yankees! I was excited. But before long, Bob was staying out late drinking, just like all the rest.

One night, Bob was out late and my mom and I got in the car to go get him. Mom said, "If he doesn't leave that bar, I'm divorcing him!" We got to the bar and she went inside. I waited in the car and soon she came back out—alone and crying. I knew what that meant.

But I was ten years old and I wanted a dad. I thought I could talk him into coming home and everything would be okay. So I went in and found Bob sitting and drinking with his buddies. With tears I pleaded, "You promised to be my dad. Please come home. Mom's going to divorce you if you don't."

Bob said, "Jay, I tell you what—if you'll get on your knees and beg me, I'll come home and be your dad." So I got down on my knees and begged. And what did Bob do? He started laughing at me. And all the other men in that bar laughed along with him.

My heart became hard after that. The tears would no longer flow. It was as if someone had turned a light off inside me. Back in the car, Mom had her own pain to deal with, and I decided I would never ask anyone for anything again.

To cope with the pain, I became the class clown in school. I was often in trouble. A few years ago my wife found an old report card with this comment by the teacher: "If Jay would spend as much time studying as he does coming up with ways to aggravate people, he would be an A student." I wanted people to notice me. Even getting punished was better than being ignored.

I blamed God for all the pain in my life, for the fact that my dad left us, for my alcoholic step-dads, for the fights and violence in our home, for the adultery that kept ripping our home apart, for the abuse that had scarred me.

By the time I became a teenager, I stopped blaming God. Why? Because I had stopped believing in God.

Two Thousand Crosses

I had seen alcohol destroy my family, and I told myself I would never let alcohol do to me what it had done to my father and to Bob. At school and in the neighborhood, I was surrounded by booze and drugs, and at first I kept my promise to myself. But at the age of twelve, with no family to go home to, I was tired of being alone. When a gang of older boys took me in, I accepted their lifestyle and had my first beer. Soon they offered me marijuana and other drugs. I didn't want to do drugs. Beer, I understood. Drugs, I didn't.

But my friends said, "You should at least find out what you're missing." So I tried one pill. Soon I was taking pills by the handful; pills of all colors, shapes and sizes. I was also smoking dope and drinking. One day I rolled up my sleeve and stuck in the first needle, and it just seemed like no big deal. Just another high.

When I was high, I felt fine. When I wasn't high, I felt like a nothing, a nobody, a kid nobody wanted. I was busted four times and spent parts of several summers in juvenile detention centers. It didn't matter what the consequences were because when I was high, I forgot about the pain of the past, even if only for a little while.

My senior year in high school, a young man in our school came back from a Christian youth retreat and he wanted everyone to know about his Jesus. The young man's name was Charlie Thompson. He'd grown up in the church, but at that retreat, he met Christ personally and his life was completely changed. He started carrying his Bible to school, and he was happy all the time. I thought he was just crazy. No one could be genuinely happy all the time—not in this life.

I had Charlie Thompson in four classes my senior year, so I couldn't get away from the guy! He kept telling me, "Jay, you need Jesus!" He gave me Christian tracts—little pamphlets. I read those tracts, and it was all new to me. I was seventeen years old and had never heard that God loved me or that Jesus died on the cross for my sins.

One day, Charlie made a mistake. He gave me a tract while I was with my buddies. I didn't mind it when he gave me tracts when it was just the two of us; I'd say, "Thanks," and I'd read it. But this time he'd embarrassed me in front of my friends—and that was unacceptable. I didn't want anyone to associate me with this crazy Charlie guy, so I publicly tore up the tract and said, "Man, get away from me with all this stuff!"

Charlie was hurt. He said, "If these guys were really your friends, they wouldn't want you to waste your life with drugs. They don't care what happens to you, but I do and Jesus does." I couldn't grasp that. Could God really care about me? Why would he? My life was a mess— even my own father didn't care about me.

Later, when no one was looking, I gathered up all the pieces of the tract I had torn up, taped it back together and read it. I didn't want anyone to know it, but I was hungry to know more.

One night, Charlie asked me to go to a Bible study with him. I said,

"Not tonight. I've got tickets to a rock concert. I'm going to see The Who."

He said, "Go ahead—but I'm praying that you have a miserable time. I'm praying that every time you see the sign of the cross somewhere, you're going to remember that Jesus nailed your sins to a cross."

I laughed it off—but during the drive to that concert, I realized for the first time in my life how much telephone poles look like crosses! I must have seen two thousand crosses on the way to that concert!

The band came out onstage, and there was Roger Daltry, the lead singer of The Who—and around his neck was the biggest gold cross I had ever seen! When the spotlight shone on that cross, it just about blinded me! I said to my buddies, "I'm gonna kill that Charlie Thompson! I'll bet he called Roger Daltry's dressing room and told him to wear that cross!"

During the concert, Daltry repeatedly used God's name in vain. I had grown up on the streets and my language was as foul as the next punk's—but for the past few weeks, I had been hearing about Jesus Christ and the price he paid on the cross. So every time I heard the name of Jesus used as a cussword, it stabbed like a knife.

I saw one of my buddies give drugs to a twelve-year-old boy, and I became furious! I threw my buddy to the ground and said, "What's the matter with you! You want this kid to end up like us?"

He said, "What do you mean? What's wrong with us?"

I said, "Man, I'm so sick of always being drunk and high and fighting with each other over nothing. I'm just sick of this empty life!"

He said, "Man, you sound like Charlie Thompson!"

And suddenly it hit me—I wanted what Charlie had been talking about. But Charlie wasn't there to tell me how to get what he had, so I just prayed to God. It was the first time I had prayed since I was six years old and I begged God to send my daddy home.

With the guitar of Pete Townsend and the voice of Roger Daltry blasting my brain, I told Jesus, "If you get me home safely, I promise I'll go to Bible study!" I knew everyone in the car, including the driver, was high on various drugs and I knew they'd be drinking all the way home. After a big concert, there were always a number of drunken crashes along "Alligator Alley," the road between Miami and Fort Myers.

Well, I made it home safely that night, and I kept my promise to God. The next night I went to a Bible study. There, I heard the greatest story ever told—that if God is for you, who could be against you? I also learned that night that it's not how you start in life, but how you finish.

The flashback of kneeling in that bar and being laughed at kept coming back to me. "How do I know God won't laugh?" I wondered. "How do I know that he won't leave me?" But he didn't laugh—and he has never left me.

It's hard to believe that a simple prayer from the heart can transform your life, but it can. In a moment of surrender I said, "Jesus, here is my messed up life. Take it." God heard me, and I was changed.

I would have never believed it myself had I not been there.

The True Meaning of Success

The best definition of "coincidence" I ever heard is this: A coincidence is when God chooses to remain anonymous. I still can't get over the amazing "coincidence" of all the crosses I saw the night Charlie Thompson told me he'd be praying for me. What were the odds that Roger Daltry would come out onstage that night wearing the biggest gold cross I have ever seen?

Offhand, I figure around six hundred to one. Shamgar odds.

And what are the odds that a kid from my background would survive all the alcohol and drugs I pumped into my body? What are the odds that I would ever make it to adulthood, let alone live a successful, fulfilled life?

What were the odds that a kid from my background would ever graduate college cum laude, earn a doctorate and build a program like Student Leadership University, which trains young people to be influential leaders?

What are the odds that a kid from my background would become an author and speaker and have the privilege of sharing a message of hope, success and fulfillment with audiences across the country and around the world?

At best, those were six-hundred-to-one odds. Shamgar odds.

You can relate to Shamgar odds as well as I can. We all face overwhelming odds in one way or another—not just when we are pursuing our grand dreams, but often when we are simply trying to survive a difficult situation. Perhaps your medical file is as thick as a phone book. Perhaps the most important relationship in your life is falling apart. Perhaps you are facing unbearable losses in your life. You feel emotionally overdrawn or even bankrupt.

You are facing Shamgar odds.

I want you to know that whatever the odds you are facing today, you don't have to be defeated. You can overcome six-hundred-to-one odds. If Shamgar could do it, if Pat Williams and Jay Strack could do it, you can do it. You can overcome Shamgar odds.

The first step in finding success in life is to hammer out a working definition of success. Three definitions have greatly affected my life. When I was twenty-one, the great motivational teacher and author Zig Ziglar befriended me. I'll never forget hearing Zig say (in a Southern drawl that's even deeper than mine), "Jay, if you want your dreams to come true, then you must be willing to help others make their dreams come true." I have watched him live that definition and have been profoundly impacted by it.

Years later, my good friend John Maxwell—the founder of the INJOY Group and author of *The 21 Irrefutable Laws of Leadership*—gave me a definition that transformed my understanding of success. He said, "Success is when those who know you the best love you the most." Now that's a startling definition, but true: Authentic success isn't about making a good public impression. To be truly successful, you must be a person of genuine integrity, character and positive influence. By that standard, only the people who know you best—your family and close friends—are qualified to say whether you are a success or a fraud.

In recent years, I have formulated a third definition of success that guides the way I live my life: *Success means saying "yes" to God's best for your life.* True success has nothing to do with your title, your fame, or your net worth. True success consists of being where God has put you, using the talent and resources God has given you and carrying out the unique mission God has assigned to you. If you say "yes" to God's best for your life, you will always be a success in God's eyes, even if this world calls you a failure.

It was only after I learned to say "yes" to God's best for my life that I experienced the privilege of traveling to over forty countries, sharing a message of hope, success and fulfillment with young people and with the leaders of such organizations as Wal-Mart, Johnson & Johnson, Chick-fil-A, the U.S. Air Force Academy and NASA. It was only after I learned to say "yes" to God's best for my life that I even had a message to share with other people.

One of the highlights of my life was when Pat Williams invited me to be the featured speaker at the chapel for the 1998 NBA All-Star Game at New York's Madison Square Garden. It was a sports fan's dream come true. I was deeply moved as I heard the various players being interviewed. Many talked about what it took to succeed and of the personal struggles they had to overcome. Some had come from crime-infested slums and had narrowly escaped the grip of gangs and drugs. As I listened to those NBA players telling their stories of triumphing over six-hundred-to-one odds, I thought back to my own battle against the odds.

The theme I was inspired to speak on that weekend was "How to Turn Your Season Around." During the days leading up to that weekend, as I prepared my talk, the story of Shamgar kept coming to mind. The three success secrets of Shamgar had turned my life around, and I knew they could have a powerful impact on the lives of those basketball stars.

The NBA All-Star Game takes place at the halfway point of the basketball season. Players are chosen based on the individual's performance and popularity, regardless of how well or how poorly their teams are doing. Some players come from teams that are heading for the play-offs, others from teams that are struggling to reach .500.

Midway through the basketball season, many players become complacent. They begin settling for what was instead of striving for what could be. A mind-set of mediocrity easily sets in. At midseason, it's not too late for a struggling team to turn on the heat and make a run for the play-offs—and it's also not too late for a dominant team to become smug and sloppy and to lose that winning edge.

So I began the chapel by asking the players this question: "What can you do to turn this season around for your team? What can one person do? Are you settling into a rut of complacency? Or are you making the most of every opportunity? You may not think your team has what it takes to win a championship this year. You may not believe that one person can do anything to turn an ordinary team into a championship team. Well, let me tell you about a man who was once in your position. His story is tucked away in a hidden corner of the Old Testament. It's the story of a man named Shamgar . . ."

And I told those NBA players about a man who saved an entire nation, armed only with an ox-goad. I told them that there were three keys to Shamgar's victory over the vastly superior forces of the Philistines. "Shamgar started where he was," I said. "He used what he had. And he did what he could."

I could see the eyes of those players light up when they heard those three principles. The concept clicked. To men whose entire careers were made up of striving, competing, struggling, winning, and yes, losing, the story of Shamgar made sense. I knew that those three principles could transform lives because they had already altered my life in a dramatic way.

Let me tell you how I first encountered the three success secrets of Shamgar.

A Purpose for My Life

I graduated from high school, an eighteen-year-old ex-junkie with hair down to my shoulders. I had spent most of my high school years in a drug-induced haze, sitting in the back row of my classrooms, rarely listening, never caring, just barely getting by. All of that changed after my life-changing encounter with Jesus Christ—thanks to the prayers and the persistent witness of Charlie Thompson.

I wanted to learn more about this God who had changed my life, so

I enrolled in a Stetson University Extension class. I will never forget one of my first sessions in an Old Testament Survey class. I scarcely knew that the Bible was divided into an Old and New Testament, and I didn't really have a clue what the class was about.

Our instructor was Dr. H. Fred Williams, who was a pastor and a father of four. He seemed every bit as much a part of the "Establishment" as I looked a part of the hippie counterculture. Yet he looked past my long hair and my ignorance of the Bible. He genuinely cared about me, listened to me and answered all of my questions. Soon, Dr. Fred not only became my teacher, but my mentor and friend.

Every Monday evening for many months, he came to the tiny apartment where I lived with my new bride, Diane. He taught us the basics of Christianity, everything from the life and teachings of Jesus of Nazareth to such principles as sharing our faith with others, giving to the church, showing compassion to the needy and trusting in God's forgiving grace instead of our own good works. Dr. Fred taught Diane and me countless truths while investing many hours in our lives. But even more important to us than what he said was the way he lived: Dr. Fred was a man of faith, intellect, integrity and compassion. Through the way he lived, he gave us a glimpse of what Jesus was like.

One day in class, as he was teaching from the book of Judges, Dr. Fred told us, "Today, I want to tell you the story about a little-known judge of Israel whose name was Shamgar. He was a farmer who went straight from the cornfield to the battlefield, where he killed six hundred Philistine warriors, armed only with a long, sharpened pole called an ox-goad."

I was profoundly impacted by Dr. Fred's conclusion: "Shamgar's life teaches us three things we should know if we're going to accomplish anything for God: first, Shamgar started where he was; second, he used what he had; and third, he did what he could. And I want you to know that God has a plan and a purpose for your life, just as he had for Shamgar. If you will start where you are, use what you have and do what you can for God, he will use you in a mighty way."

Wow! I thought. *God could actually use me? He would want to work through me?* I could hardly believe it—and I couldn't stop thinking about those three simple principles.

After the class was over, I sat down with Dr. Fred and asked him question after question: "You mean God has a purpose for my life? Me? Jay Strack? You mean God actually wants to do great things through my life? But why? There's nothing special about me. I'm not talented, I'm not a good student, I haven't lived a good life, I've been really messed up! How could God use someone like me?"

But then Dr. Fred reminded me about his own early life. When he was a baby, no more than two or three months old, he was found in a cardboard box on the doorstep of the Porter-Leath Orphanage in Memphis, Tennessee. He was adopted by a poor but loving couple from Mississippi and raised in a tiny rural "shotgun house"—a long, narrow house, one room wide and three rooms deep, so-named because you can fire a shotgun through the front door and the shot will pass out the back door without ever hitting a wall. Dr. Fred served in the navy in World War II and was severely wounded in Okinawa in 1944. He spent two years in VA hospitals, undergoing numerous skin grafts and operations to save his leg.

So Dr. Fred had earned the right to talk to me about how to overcome long odds. He had started life with two strikes against him and had gone through crippling adversity, yet God was using him in a mighty way. He insisted that I was exactly the kind of person God uses—an ordinary guy with a messed-up past and no confidence in the future. He told me that Moses started out that way, and so did the disciples of Jesus.

And, of course, so did Shamgar. He was just a farmer with a big stick in his hand, and God used him to save a nation. "You never know what God can do through you," he told me, "until you trust him to let him have his way in your life."

So I decided to do exactly that. I was going to trust God and see what he wanted to do through me. I went back to the apartment and told Diane what Dr. Fred had told me, and she was completely captivated by the idea of God working through our lives. So we began to pray together that God would use us and lead us.

Over the next few days, I started thinking about the Shamgar principles: Start where you are, use what you have, do what you can. Wherever I was, whatever I was doing, I'd think, "Start where you are." Where was I? I might be in the checkout stand at the grocery store or on the steps of the library. Then I'd think, "Use what you have." What did I have? I had a story—my own story about how I had first encountered Jesus Christ. Then I'd think, "Do what you can." What could I do? Well, I could tell my story.

So that's what I did. Wherever I happened to be, I began telling my story to anyone and everyone who might be in earshot. Some people walked away. Others ran away. Some stayed and listened. A few considered what I had to say, and they had an encounter with Jesus Christ, too.

Time passed, and Dr. Fred said to me, "I'd like you to go to a little church on the edge of the Everglades and tell your story to the people there." So I drove down to that little white church, ready to tell my story. I walked in with hair down to my shoulders, with Diane beside me in her hippie dress. There were seventeen people in the pews, and I got up in front of them and told them the story of how I had encountered Jesus Christ.

The people were shocked by our appearance—but they were even more shocked by the fact that God had blessed my message. After the church service, one of the deacons asked me to come back. I called Dr. Fred and he helped me come up with another message from my Old Testament study class. After my second visit to that church, those seventeen people had a meeting. When the meeting was over, they asked me to be the pastor of their church!

I felt totally unqualified. I had never been to seminary and barely had a year of college under my belt—yet these people wanted me to be their pastor! What should I do?

Then I remembered that I had prayed and asked God to use me and work through my life. I had already made a decision that I was going to start where I was, use what I had and do what I could. These people were asking me to start in that little church, use what little speaking ability and Bible knowledge I had (which was almost nil!) and do what I could. How could I say no?

So week after week, I got up in the pulpit of that tiny church and preached my sermons in my own stumbling way. I repeatedly went to Dr. Fred for advice and encouragement, and he patiently mentored and guided me. A year later, our little church had baptized 110 people. I couldn't believe what God had done! And I knew that it was all God's work, because I didn't have the skills, knowledge or educational background to do such a thing in my own strength.

As it turned out, that was just the beginning of an adventure with God that has continued for thirty years. The kid who once got kicked out of the classroom has had the privilege of walking into boardrooms of leading corporations, sharing the stage with national politicians, and delivering messages of inspiration and motivation to NFL teams such as the Miami Dolphins, the Dallas Cowboys, the Tampa Bay

Buccaneers, the Green Bay Packers, and the Pittsburgh Steelers. The kid who was once turned down by thirteen colleges has now addressed the faculty and students of 145 universities. The kid nobody would pay any attention to has now spoken before thousands of audiences totaling more than fifteen million people.

How was that possible? Because one man, Dr. H. Fred Williams, looked at a long-haired former drug abuser and said, "Jay, God wants to use you. He wants to work through you to demonstrate his power to other people. And all you have to do is start where you are, use what you have and do what you can."

The Man from Sweet Home

A few years later, I began my own career in Christian ministry. I had the privilege of being on the speaking platform with a man named E. V. Hill. That day, Dr. Hill spoke about Shamgar—this same obscure judge of ancient Israel whom I had first heard about from my professor, Dr. H. Fred Williams. While Dr. Fred had taught me those three principles in his wise, warm, quiet manner, Dr. E. V. Hill pounded them into my heart with thunder and lightning! He was one of the most powerful preachers I have ever heard. I can still hear his voice ringing in my memory: "Shamgar did what he could, with what he had, right where he was—and every chance he got!"

And who was Dr. E. V. Hill? Like Shamgar, he was a man who overcame six-hundred-to-one odds, a man who triumphed over obstacles and adversity. E. V. Hill said "yes" to God's best for his life—and he impacted countless lives for God.

Edward Victor Hill was born into poverty and raised in a little log cabin at the edge of Sweet Home in southeast Texas. He was one of five kids born to a single mom during the Great Depression. Hill was also mothered by a woman who was no relation to him, though he always called her "Momma." When he was eleven years old, Momma led him in a prayer in which he gave his life to Jesus Christ.

When E. V. was in the ninth grade, Momma stood up in church and told the congregation, "My boy E. V. is going to finish high school." It was an unusual prophecy for those Depression-era days. Few African American boys finished school in those days; most dropped out and got low-paying jobs. But E. V. graduated, just as Momma said he would.

Momma also promised E. V. that he would go to college—and that was even more unheard-of! When he graduated from high school, Momma bought him some new clothes and a bus ticket. She took him to the bus station and gave him five dollars. "I'll be praying for you," she told him as she put him on the bus. The bus took him to Prairie View, northeast of Houston. He spent most of the five dollars on bus fare and arrived at the campus of Prairie View A&M with only $1.58 in his pocket.

He got in line to register for classes—then he saw a sign that informed him that all new students had to pay $83 in cash at the time of registration. What should he do? He was about to step out of line and walk away when he heard Momma's voice in his mind, saying, "I'll be praying for you." He figured he didn't have anything to lose by standing in line a few minutes longer. When he reached the front of the line and gave his name, the registrar said, "You're Ed Hill? Our office has been trying to contact you. The university wants to offer you a four-year scholarship—tuition, room and board, and a $35 a month expense allowance." E. V. Hill knew that God had led him to that university. Again he remembered Momma's words: "I'll be praying for you."

E. V. Hill finished college, got married and began preaching, but the church couldn't pay him enough to live on. Against the advice of his wife, Jane, E. V. pooled what little money they had and used it to buy a service station. Jane insisted that he didn't have the experience or the time to run a service station, but E. V. said he knew what he was doing. Within months, the service station went broke. Hill lost his investment.

When he went home and told Jane about it, he expected her to say, "I told you so." Instead, she said, "Ed, I've been thinking this over, and I figured out that if you were a drinking man and a smoking man, you would have spent as much on liquor and tobacco as you did on that service station. At least you lost that money honestly, trying to do some good. So let's just forget it ever happened."

In 1963, E. V. Hill was called as pastor of the Mount Zion Missionary Baptist Church, right in the heart of the troubled Watts section of south-central Los Angeles. He served as the pastor of Mount Zion for the next forty-two years. He gained the respect of everyone in the community, including the street gangs, and he frequently mediated disputes between rival factions. He even spearheaded a street-level peace movement called "The Moratorium on Gang Murder."

Under his leadership, Mount Zion became a hub of political activism and social compassion in the center of Los Angeles. On one occasion, Dr. Billy Graham showed up unannounced, just to hear E. V. Hill preach. On another occasion, President George H. W. Bush visited the church while the streets of south-central Los Angeles were still smoking from the 1992 riots.

A fiery preacher and a committed evangelist, E. V. Hill spoke to audiences around the world. Untold thousands responded to his message of God's love for sinners. He was such a committed student of the Bible that you could give him practically any reference—such as John 14:6 or Malachi 3:2 or 2 Timothy 3:16—and he could deliver a polished, eloquent sermon on the spot.

Early in his career, E. V. Hill became deeply involved in the fight for racial justice through nonviolent resistance. He joined with Dr. Martin Luther King, Jr., and other African American pastors to form the Southern Christian Leadership Conference. A liberal Democrat as a young man, a conservative Republican in his maturity, E. V. Hill transcended distinctions of left and right and focused on bringing people together. He has been a featured speaker at both the Republican and Democratic national conventions.

He was a close friend of Dr. Billy Graham for most of his life and served as associate professor of evangelism for the Billy Graham Evangelistic Association. In 1971, Dr. Graham took E. V. Hill and seven other black clergymen to the White House to meet privately with President Richard Nixon about race relations. In 1973, he gave the prayer at President Nixon's second inauguration—quite an accomplishment for a man who was born in a log cabin in Sweet Home, Texas.

Hitting the Devil

In Los Angeles, E. V. Hill founded "The Lord's Kitchen," a program that has fed more than two million homeless people without a dime of government money. He was also a member of President Reagan's Task Force on Private Sector Initiative.

In the 1990s, E. V. Hill became a featured speaker at Promise Keepers men's rallies around the nation. Here's a typical passage from an E. V. Hill Promise Keepers' message:

> *Jesus came back at Satan and said, "Devil, It is written, 'Man shall not live by bread alone.' It is written, 'Thou shalt not tempt the Lord thy God.'" Jesus hit the devil over and over and over with Scripture! And you know*

what happened? The devil ran! And guess what you can do, beginning tonight? You don't have to take it from the devil! You don't have to take his mess! You don't have to take his stuff! Hit him! Hit him! Hit him!

E. V. Hill's turbocharged preaching would invariably pull fifty thousand men to their feet, shouting right along, "Hit him! Hit him! *Hit him!*" You wouldn't want to be the devil in a stadium full of Promise Keepers while E. V. Hill was preaching!

During the last year of his ministry, Dr. Hill continued ministering despite a diabetic condition that had so weakened his legs that he had to sit down while he preached. On February 8, 2003, he was admitted to Cedars-Sinai Medical Center in Los Angeles with an aggressive form of pneumonia. He died on February 24.

When I think of Shamgar, I think of E. V. Hill—a man who came out of nowhere, from a little place called Sweet Home, Texas, just a few miles south of Sublime and a little north of Hope. But E. V. Hill started where he was. He was raised in poverty, and he set off for college with nothing but pocket change for spending money. He didn't have much, but he used what he had. There weren't many opportunities for a young black man in southeast Texas during the Great Depression. But E. V. Hill did what he could.

Starting where he was, using what he had, doing what he could, Dr. Hill became a friend of the poor and a counselor to presidents. He marched with Dr. King, and demanded that justice roll down like mighty waters. He fed the hungry and brought peace to warring neighborhoods. He brought the refreshing message of Jesus to thirsty souls.

So these are the two men who taught me the most about the three success secrets of Shamgar—Dr. H. Fred Williams and Dr. E. V. Hill. Those three simple principles changed the direction of my life. Over the years, I have shared these principles with young men and women at the Student Leadership University, with business executives and academicians, with political leaders and just plain folk. And these principles click. They change lives and revolutionize organizations.

That's what this book is about: one person making a difference in the world through God's power by following these three simple secrets:

1. Start where you are.
2. Use what you have.
3. Do what you can.

In the rest of this book, you are going to become very well acquainted with Shamgar and his three success secrets. My friend Pat Williams and I have written chapters on each of the three principles, plus we have interspersed a fictional narrative of Shamgar's story.

Obviously, our version of Shamgar's story is conjectural. We don't know whether Shamgar had a family or not, nor do we know for sure how he accomplished this incredible feat of killing six hundred Philistines with an ox-goad. We've invented names, scenes and personalities, yet every aspect of our fictional narrative is plausible and consistent with what we know about Shamgar's life and times. We hope that this fictional story will bring the reality of this ancient man to life in your imagination.

So join us in an adventure of discovery as we journey through these three life-changing principles from the story of Shamgar. The three success secrets of Shamgar have transformed Pat's life and mine. We know that you can live a transformed life as well through these three simple, yet profound, principles.

Read on. We'll show you how.

The First Secret:
Start Where
You Are

The Tale of Shamgar: Part One

Shamgar crouched statue-still in the shadows at the edge of the cedar grove. His right hand gripped a spearlike shaft of wood. His eyes were fixed on the animal that moved silently through the dappled sunlight just a dozen yards before him: a male fallow deer.

The deer's head was crowned with a pair of forked antlers. Its eyes were brown and shining, and its reddish-brown coat was dotted with white. The deer sniffed the breeze—

And *froze*.

Shamgar instinctively flexed his right arm, weighing the balance of the wooden shaft, which was tipped with iron at both ends. *He knows I'm near,* he thought, *but he doesn't see me.* He waited for just the right moment—

Now!

In a single swift motion, Shamgar rose from his crouch and hurled the wooden shaft. The startled deer leaped forward—but the man had plenty of experience hunting deer with an ox-goad. He had aimed slightly ahead of the deer—and the deer had leaped into the bull's-eye. The whizzing shaft penetrated between the second and third ribs. The deer tumbled to the grass with the deadly shaft pointed at the sky.

When Shamgar reached the deer, the creature was already dead. He knelt beside the animal and stroked its smooth coat. "You died bravely, *Tzvi*," he said soothingly. "Rest well. My family will feed on your strength." Shamgar was a farmer and a hunter. He had a deep respect for living things, especially those that gave up their lives to keep his family strong.

He took his ox-goad out of the deer's thorax and used the chisel-shaped end to scoop out a shallow hole in the soft ground. Then he cut the carcass open with the iron knife he kept tucked into his belt. He gutted the deer, poured the blood and innards into the hole and covered it with dirt. Shamgar was a devout man, and the Law of God said that anyone who hunts and kills an animal must drain it and bury the blood in the earth, because, said the Law, "the life of every creature is its blood."

Shamgar draped the carcass of the deer over his broad shoulders and loped along the winding footpath. About a mile ahead, just over the next two hills, was the farm of his friend Reuel. A deer this size was too much meat for one family, and Shamgar and Reuel often shared with each other when they hunted. Reuel and Shamgar had been like brothers since boyhood, and Reuel's wife, Yael, had cared for Shamgar's wife, Dara, two winters before when she was sick and nearly died.

As he walked, Shamgar talked with his God. He spoke aloud, as one would speak to a friend who was walking alongside. He thanked God for the warm meat he carried on his shoulders, for the hot sunshine on his face and arms, and for the cool breeze that ruffled his long black hair.

He was down in the swale between the two hills when he caught a whiff of smoke on the breeze. Not camp smoke, not the smoke of burning wood. Something about this smoke warned him of danger. His pace quickened. Then he saw it rise before him from the far side of the hill—billows of black smoke.

It was coming from Reuel's farm. Shamgar's lope turned to a sprint.

There was a stand of oak trees along the crest of the hill. Shamgar turned aside, sprinted off the path and into the shadow of the oaks. Ash-laden smoke swirled and eddied through the oak grove from the valley below.

Still gripping the ox-goad in his right fist, Shamgar took the deer from his shoulders and dropped the carcass at the gnarled foot of an ancient oak. Then, bending low, he crept up behind a tree and peered into the valley.

A blaze was spreading through Reuel's wheat field.

It was early in the month of Sivan, and the time for harvesting wheat was just a week or two away. The swaying grain was golden, almost ready for the sickle—and now it was going up in flames.

Shamgar's keen eyes pierced the smoky air. There were men with torches walking through the field—outlanders, not Hebrews. He quickly counted a dozen men. From the look of them, they were not from one of the neighboring Canaanite tribes. They had come from a distance.

Sunlight glinted off their heavy armor. Cruel swords hung from their belts. From the top of the hill, Shamgar could not make out their features—but he could see dark splashes on their coarse tunics.

The life of every creature is its blood.

He looked to the far end of the field, where a little square farmhouse made of stone stood. Shamgar had helped Reuel place the stones and build the walls of that house. Where was his friend? Where was Reuel's wife, Yael? Where were their two sons? Something hard and cold, like a fist made of iron, clutched at Shamgar's heart.

A holy rage surged in his blood, though his mind remained clear. "God of Abraham, Isaac and Jacob," he said, "make my arm strong. Be my shield and my strength." Then he dashed, crouching, down the hill toward the flaming field.

Toward the enemy.

Shamgar kept the smoke and flames of the burning field between himself and the outlanders. They were laughing and shouting to each other in a coarse, heathen tongue. Shamgar dived into the waves of wheat, circling around the advancing flames, moving toward one of the men who was walking along the edge of the field, torching the grain. The flames roared and crackled, weaving braids of fire and smoke in the air. The heat roasted Shamgar's skin, but he didn't feel it.

The man with the torch was just a few yards from him now. He wore no helmet. Shamgar rose up behind him and swung the chisel-end of the ox-goad. It struck the man's head with a sound like a mallet on wood. The stunned man dropped facedown, crushing stalks of wheat with his heavy body. In the next instant, Shamgar brought the other end of the ox-goad to bear. The outlander died quickly.

In the next instant, Shamgar was down in a crouch, hidden by the wheat, the smoke and the flames. The other outlanders had not seen him kill their brother. They were still shouting and laughing, unaware that they were hunted men.

Shamgar knew he would have to act before the fires burned away his cover. Four of the outlanders were in a knot together at the far end of the field. The others were scattered about the field. He selected his targets and moved through the swaying grain. Those without helmets he stunned first, then speared, as he had done to the first man. The men with helmets had to be silenced before they could shout and warn the others, so Shamgar targeted their throats.

Within minutes, Shamgar had sent eight evil men to their Maker. The remaining four had still taken no notice of their dwindling numbers. The smoke and flames had provided Shamgar with the cover he needed. Then—

"Akimolok! Hakuzzok!"

Outlander names, called out by the commander of the armored men. He called the names casually. There was no note of urgency or concern in the man's voice. Not yet.

Seconds passed. The dead men did not answer. The commander called again.

"Akimolok! Hakuzzok!" A pause. "Nobkah! Rakkah! Nashikh!"

Still, the dead did not answer. The commander called again, and this time his voice was full of urgency—and fear. His men had gone out to torch a field of wheat. The field was burning, but the men had vanished. Again and again, the commander called, and still no one answered.

Ox-goad in hand, Shamgar crept closer.

The outlanders babbled to each other in their profane tongue. One was practically shrieking. Shamgar couldn't understand the words, but he understood fear. "God of Abraham, Isaac and Jacob," he hissed between clenched teeth, "grant me the strength to do your will. Deliver these outlanders into my hand."

Then he bellowed a shout of war!

The outlanders heard it and broke into a run, dashing through a thicket of shrubs and bramble toward an oak grove that spread along a nearby hillside. Keeping low, Shamgar followed quickly.

The outlanders' armor clanked loudly as they ran. They cursed and swore, and their footsteps thudded heavily. Shamgar pursued them like a silent shadow moving through the trees. He could see them, but they couldn't see him.

Shamgar's ox-goad sang through the air, and the last man fell with a scream. His fellows ran all the harder and didn't look back. Moments passed. Another man fell with an ox-goad standing straight up between his shoulder blades. Shamgar snatched it out of the fallen man's back without breaking his stride. Moments later, another outlander fell.

Only one man left—the commander. He had outrun all of his men. Shamgar shouted to the man and ordered him to halt. Though the outlander did not understand Hebrew, he slowed his stride, looked over his shoulder and stopped. He was alone—but he saw that his pursuer was also alone.

And his pursuer didn't even have a proper weapon! No sword, no shield, no armor—just an ox-goad! The man who stood before him was nothing but a peasant farmer! Cursing himself for running from a mere peasant, the commander drew his sword and charged at Shamgar.

With a quick prayer on his lips, Shamgar swung the chisel end of the ox-goad, batting the outlander's sword aside. Then he whirled the point around and plunged it deep—and pulled it back.

The outlander was wide-eyed with surprise. The sword slipped from his fingers and clanked at his feet. He fell facedown in the dirt. His body shuddered, and he breathed no more.

Shamgar turned the body over for a closer look. The outlander wore an amulet in the shape of a fish rising out of the waves. It was an amulet of Dagon, the fish-god of the Philistines.

Now Shamgar knew who his enemy was.

When he returned to the burning fields and the desolate stone farmhouse, Shamgar found four Hebrew bodies. When he saw what the Philistines had done to Reuel and to his wife and two sons, Shamgar tore his clothes and fell upon the body of his friend. His cry of grief echoed in the hills.

Shamgar wept until the fire in the field had burned itself out, and his skin and hair were dusted white with ashes.

3

Start Here, Start Now

by Pat Williams

Alvin C. York was the Shamgar of World War I.

Born in a log cabin in the tiny village of Pall Mall, Tennessee, in 1887, Alvin helped his father on the farm and spent a lot of time hunting in the woods. As a teenager, Alvin gained a reputation as a deadly marksman. He could plug the eye of a turkey at a hundred yards.

But as Alvin York moved through his late teens and into his twenties, he developed a reputation as a hell-raiser. The townspeople of Pall Mall agreed that Alvin would never amount to anything. He had a definite taste for whiskey, gambling, brawling in bars and the wrong kind of girls. It had been a very long time since he had darkened the door of the church.

All of that changed suddenly in 1914 when Alvin's best friend, Everett Delk, was killed in a bar fight just over the state line, in Static, Kentucky. Suddenly, Alvin was brought face-to-face with the brevity of life and the reality of death. Soon afterward, he astonished his neighbors when he walked into a revival meeting where the Rev. H. H. Russell of the Church of Christ in Christian Union was preaching. At the end of the service, when

Brother Russell invited people to come forward and give their lives to Christ, Alvin walked forward.

Immediately, Alvin York was a changed young man. The Church of Christ in Christian Union was a strict sect with congregations in only three states—Tennessee, Kentucky and Ohio. Church members adhered to stringent rules of behavior: no drinking, dancing, swimming, swearing, going to movies or reading trashy books. Oh, and one more thing: no violence or killing, even as a soldier in war. Alvin was baptized and joined the church, becoming a Sunday school teacher and the church choir leader. In the church, he met the young woman he would later marry, Gracie Williams.

Alvin's commitment to the church's strict rules was severely tested when the United States declared war on Germany in 1917. Alvin received a draft notice, which he returned to the draft board with these words scrawled across the back: "Don't want to fight." He was denied conscientious objector status because his church was not a recognized pacifist sect, like the Quakers or Mennonites. He reported to Camp Gordon, Georgia, and went through basic training, where he astonished his superiors with his ability as a marksman. Still, he stubbornly insisted that he would never aim his rifle at another human being.

After a series of long talks with his battalion commander, George Buxton, Alvin York was persuaded that war, though horrible and tragic, was sometimes a moral necessity in order to free innocent people from tyranny. So he reluctantly agreed to fight for his country. With a rank of corporal, Alvin York was shipped to France in the spring of 1918. For the next few months, the 82nd Division occupied a sector behind the lines and saw no action. Then, on September 12, Alvin York's division engaged the Germans in the St. Mihiel campaign, fighting ably and advancing quickly.

In early October, York's division was sent to support the Meuse-Argonne offensive. On October 8, Corporal York and sixteen other soldiers were on a predawn mission under the command of Sergeant Bernard Early. Their mission was to seize the railroad near Chatel-Chehery. Following a map that was printed in French instead of English, they got lost and found themselves behind enemy lines. York and his fellow soldiers exchanged fire with the much larger German force—and within minutes, the Germans surprised the Americans by surrendering! The enemy soldiers had mistakenly thought themselves outnumbered.

Soon, the Germans realized they had surrendered too soon, and some machine gunners on a nearby ridge opened fire on the Americans. Alvin looked around and saw his fellow soldiers scream and crumple to the ground, riddled by machine-gun fire. York's best friend in the army, Murray Savage, lay dying a few yards away. Sergeant Early lay mortally wounded, bleeding profusely from three bullet wounds.

Two corporals, Harry Parsons and William Cutting, took charge and ordered York to go up the ridge and silence the machine gun. In his journal, Alvin York recalled what happened next:

> As soon as the machine guns opened fire on me, I began to exchange shots with them. There were over thirty [German soldiers in the machine-gun nest, keeping the gun firing continuously], and all I could do was touch the Germans off just as fast as I could. I was sharpshooting. I don't think I missed a shot. It was no time to miss.
>
> In order to sight me or to swing their machine guns on me, the Germans had to show their heads above the trench, and every time I saw a head I just touched it off. All the time I kept yelling at them to come down. I didn't want to kill any more than I had to. But it was they or I. And I was giving them the best I had.

Suddenly a German officer and five men jumped out of the trench and charged me with fixed bayonets. I changed to the old automatic and just touched them off too. I touched off the sixth man first, then the fifth, then the fourth, then the third and so on. I wanted them to keep coming.

I didn't want the rear ones to see me touching off the front ones. I was afraid they would drop down and pump a volley into me.

I got hold of the German major, and he told me if I wouldn't kill any more of them he would make them quit firing. So I told him all right, if he would do it now. So he blew a little whistle, and they quit shooting and came down and gave up.

By the time the smoke had cleared, Alvin York and the nine remaining men in his unit had captured 132 German prisoners. For his heroism under fire, York was awarded the Congressional Medal of Honor. He returned home to Pall Mall, married Gracie Williams, and they lived in a home that was given to them by the Nashville Rotarians.

Why did I tell you this story? Because Alvin C. York reminds me so much of Shamgar. Alvin *started where he was*—the little Podunk town of Pall Mall, Tennessee. He *used what he had*—an amazing ability to shoot the eye out of a turkey or "touch off" a German machine gunner. He *did what he could*—walking right into a squad of German soldiers who were charging at him with fixed bayonets.

You see, I know that some people think that the story of Shamgar is nothing more than a wild myth. After all, how could one man defeat six hundred sword-wielding Philistines when he was armed with only a sharpened pole? How could one man overcome six-hundred-to-one odds and save his entire nation from destruction? But is the story of Shamgar really so hard to believe?

Alvin York faced a machine-gun nest that swarmed with thirty

German soldiers. He took on six charging Germans with fixed bayonets. He and his nine fellow soldiers captured 132 German prisoners alive and marched them back to their own lines. This is a historical fact—and so is the story of Shamgar.

I don't want you to think that in telling either the story of Shamgar or the story of Alvin York, I'm glorifying killing or war. I believe that war is an evil thing—but sometimes it's a necessary evil. And I say this as a father who has two sons in the U.S. Marine Corps, one of whom fought in Iraq.

I see both Alvin York and Shamgar as reluctant warriors—men who took no pleasure in killing, but who fought in a just cause to save innocent lives. More importantly, I believe that the story of Shamgar has a great deal to teach us about how we can live a more effective and meaningful life.

"When I Get More Time . . ."

Ultimately, the only way to find meaning in life is to live a life that counts for God—a life like that of Shamgar. You must start where you are, use what you have and do what you can. So let's take a closer look at what it means to "start where you are."

Shamgar started where he was—out on a farm in Palestine. He never got to go to one of the big universities in Alexandria, Damascus or Nineveh. He never got to study battlefield tactics in one of the great military academies of Babylon or Assyria. He was a simple farmer who used a pair of oxen to plow his fields on a ranch outside of West Overshoe, just over the hill from Box Springs.

Wherever "here" is, that's where you've got to start. If you're in Paris, Texas, there's no point in saying, "I want to start in Paris, France." If you have a dream or a calling to fulfill, don't wait until you can get to the Big City. Start building now, right where you are. Start planning, preparing, creating and constructing. Start here, start now.

When is the best time to plant a fruit tree? Twenty years ago! But when is the *second* best time? Right now! You can't undo yesterday, but you can start where you are, and you can start today.

People often think, "Someday, when I have more time, I'm going to make my dreams come true," or, "Someday, when I get off this farm and move to the big city, I'm going to accomplish great things." If that had been Shamgar's attitude, the Jewish people would all be speaking Philistine today.

Shamgar never said, "I'll defend Israel from the Philistines *someday*—maybe when I can find someone to go with me, or when I have saved up enough to buy a bigger ox-goad." Shamgar didn't wait for "someday." He picked up his ox-goad and got right to it. He started where he was, and he started at that very moment.

There is no telling how much more effective and successful you and I could be if we could grasp the importance of the Sacred Now, this very moment of time that is, and that will never be again. Yet Shamgar understood it well. He lived in the Sacred Now. He acted in the Sacred Now. He refused to waste the Sacred Now.

What do you want to do someday? Don't wait. Start now. Don't put off living. Live now.

How do you want to be remembered after you're gone? How do you want your obituary to read? Well, here's a sobering thought: You are writing your obituary right now. Think of all the things you want people to read about your life when you're gone. Those are the things you need to be doing right now, while you're still here. As playwright George Bernard Shaw once observed, "If you take too long in deciding what to do with your life, you'll find you've already done it."

Few of us believe in Santa Claus or the Tooth Fairy, but most of us believe in a far more ridiculous myth—the myth of "When I get more time." As in, "When I get more time, I'm going to write that novel." Or, "When I get more time, I'm going to start my own Internet business." Or, "When I get more time, I'm going to volunteer at the local homeless shelter."

Why do you think you're ever going to have more time than you have right now? Does that bestselling novelist you applaud, that successful entrepreneur you envy, those selfless volunteers you admire have one more minute in their days than you do? Do you think John Grisham, Bill Gates and Mother Teresa had extra-capacity wristwatches that hold more hours than yours? Fact is, every human being on this planet gets exactly sixty minutes per hour, twenty-four hours per day, same as every other human being.

So if you're waiting until you get more time, you have a long wait ahead of you. If you want to get anything accomplished before you die, then you must start here and start now. Don't "find time"—*make* time. That means you have to prioritize. You have to quit doing what doesn't count and start doing the very thing that is most important to you. And you must *do it now.*

John C. Maxwell, author of *The 21 Irrefutable Laws of Leadership,* told me of a man he once heard about—a man who, at the age of fifty-five, had learned the true value of time. One day, this man sat down and did the math. Assuming a life span of seventy-five years and fifty-two weeks in a year, he punched these numbers into his calculator: 75 x 52 = 3,900.

What did that tell him? It told him that, in an average lifetime, he could expect to have 3,900 Saturdays to do with as he pleased. He could work on those Saturdays to make extra money, or he could use them to do some project he had always wanted to do, or he could enjoy those Saturdays with his family.

Then it hit him: "I'm fifty-five years old! I've already used up most of those 3,900 Saturdays!" Again he tapped some numbers into his calculator, whereupon he discovered that over 2,800 of his lifetime allotment of Saturdays had already been used up! He had only a thousand or so Saturdays left to spend! He decided he had better use them wisely.

So this man went out and bought a thousand marbles, one for every Saturday he had left, assuming a normal life span. He put the marbles in a clear plastic jar in his den. Then, every Saturday morning, he took one marble out of the jar and tossed it in the trash. He found that, week by week, as he watched the marbles diminish, he was able to focus his mind on the things that truly mattered in life. He could literally see his life draining out of that jar like sand falling through an hourglass—and that visual reminder of the brevity of life motivated him to get the priorities of his life in proper order.

Johnny Hunt pastors a large church in the suburbs of Atlanta. I once heard him observe, "Don't be paralyzed by the past nor hypnotized by the future. Stay riveted on the present moment. It's the key to your success."

As sales and marketing guru Paul J. Meyer once said, "Most time is wasted not in hours but in minutes. A bucket with a small hole in the bottom gets just as empty as a bucket that is deliberately poured out." And automaker Henry Ford once observed, "Most people get ahead during the time that others waste." It's true: Your time is your life. When you waste time, you waste a piece of your life.

According to an ancient Jewish legend, King Solomon once had his goldsmith fashion a ring and inscribe the band with words that would be fitting for all occasions and situations. The goldsmith did as the king directed. He created a beautiful golden ring and presented it to King Solomon. The king took the ring and examined the inscription on the band. It read: "This, too, shall pass."

King Solomon was baffled by the inscription, but he admired the ring and wore it every day. Some days were bad days, full of troubling news and woe. He might have to send out troops to battle Hittite raiders on the border or settle an argument between two of the concubines in his harem. On such days, he would read the inscription on his ring—"This, too, shall pass"—and be comforted.

On other days, he would get news that a rich vein of gold had just been struck in one of his mines, or he would get a visit from that gorgeous Queen of Sheba, and he'd think, "Life doesn't get much better than this!" Just then, he would notice the inscription on his ring— "This, too, shall pass"—and he'd be sobered.

That ring truly did fit every occasion, and the inscription kept his mind focused on the fact that nothing lasts forever—neither bad times, nor good. The important thing was to make the most of whatever time he had, because, "This, too, shall pass."

This very moment that you now inhabit is a sacred moment, the Sacred Now. It is a holy gift entrusted to you by God. This moment, this heartbeat, is in your hands, and you may do with it what you will—but once it is spent, you will never get it back.

You may say, "Well, I'm not really free in how I use my time. I have responsibilities, obligations, a family, a career and hundreds of details I have to deal with, from showering and getting dressed to working at the office to dealing with the flat tire on my car. All of these things take time, and when I get them all done, I don't have any time left for the things I really wish I could do."

Granted, there are many things we must do to maintain our lives and take care of our families. But is it really true that you couldn't find one hour out of twenty-four to devote to that project or goal or dream that you've been putting off? You couldn't spend one less hour in front of the television or the computer? You couldn't skip one lunch hour or get up one hour earlier in the morning?

Someone once said, "Most of us spend our lives as if we had another one in the bank." Is that the way you've been living your life? Have you been letting life slip away from you as you marked time, killed time, wasted time? Every second of your life is irreversible. Every heartbeat is irreplaceable. Every Sacred Now is an opportunity that, once lost, will never come again.

Neil Armstrong, the first human being to set foot on the moon, wisely said, "I believe every human has a finite number of heartbeats. I don't intend to waste any of mine." And poet Carl Sandburg observed, "Time is the coin of your life. It is the only coin you have, and only you can determine how it will be spent. Be careful, lest you let other people spend it for you."

No Time in a Bottle

If you've been around as long as I have, you probably remember the songs of singer-songwriter Jim Croce. He grew up in South Philly, watching performers like Fats Domino and the Coasters on TV's American Bandstand. He looked like a tough guy, but everyone who knew him said he had a big, warm, fun-loving heart.

Jim Croce spent the first decade of his adult life toiling in a series of day jobs: teaching emotionally disturbed children, working in a hospital, driving trucks, operating a jackhammer at construction sites. At night, he would sing and play guitar in coffeehouses. He wasn't waiting for his "big break"—he was hustling for it.

When he was twenty-nine, Jim Croce finally landed his first recording contract. His first album, *You Don't Mess Around With Jim,* was completed quickly, many of the songs being recorded in just one or two takes. Once the album was released, Croce's music, an acoustic blend of folk and rock, caught on fast. The first two singles released from that album quickly became number one hits on AM radio, and Jim Croce became a star. His long-delayed dream had finally come true.

His first two hits were upbeat, honky-tonk rock ballads. His record company decided to release a third song from the album—a soft, plaintive song called "Time in a Bottle." It was about how precious each moment of life is, and how quickly those moments pass, never to come again. The song wistfully recounted the things Croce would do if only he could keep time in a bottle and pour out a few extra hours whenever he needed them.

Before "Time in a Bottle" could be released, Jim Croce proved that the words of that song were truer than he realized. On September 20, 1973, after performing in concert at Northwestern State University in Natchitoches, Louisiana, Croce boarded a small chartered plane along with a flight crew and members of his band. The heavily loaded plane clipped a tree as it took off. Like Croce's career, the plane had barely gotten off the ground before it crashed. Jim Croce was dead at age thirty.

We can't save time in a bottle—and we never know how much time we have left. We tend to think about "the rest of our lives" in terms of years and decades. The truth is, "the rest of our lives" might be measured in hours or even minutes. So we need to make the most of each moment we have.

Don't wait to start your life. Accept the fact that it has already started, and it is moving along at a rate of sixty seconds per minute, sixty minutes per hour. You can't slow those minutes down. You can only use them wisely, spending them on the things you care about most.

It's foolish to say, "When I retire, I'll start living," or, "When I finish school, I'll start living," or, "When I lose twenty pounds, I'll start living," or, "When I get more time, I'll start living." You are living now. You are spending one Sacred Now after another, even as you are reading these words. The question is, when you reach the very last Now of your earthly life, when your heart beats for the very last time, will you know that your life has been well spent and well invested in the things that matter—or will you regret all of the wasted Nows that once were and will never come again?

The great evangelist Dr. Billy Graham once said, "You possess a non-renewable resource, which is headed toward total depletion, and that resource is time. You can either invest your life, or let it dribble through your fingers like sands in an hourglass. If there is ever a time to redeem every second, every minute, it is now. You may never have tomorrow. You can't count your days but, with the Lord as your Savior, you can make your days count."

Marilyn Allen is a literary agent and publishing consultant with Diforio, Allen, O'Shea Literary Partners. She once said, "The days are long. The years are short." So concisely stated—and so true. Our days seem long, busy and packed with so many things to do—yet we turn around at the end of the year and it all seems like a blur, a whole year spent in a flash. And we wonder what we have to show for it.

We need to become more conscious of the fact that we have a finite supply of heartbeats, a finite supply of seconds, a limited number of opportunities to truly inhabit the moment and live our lives. So we have to begin at the moment we swing our legs over the edge of the bed and plant our feet upon the floor. We have to make a commitment to ourselves: "The next twenty-four hours are a gift from God, and I will use them to do things of value and significance."

How do we carry out that commitment? By beginning each morning with a plan. In my own life, I do this by ending each day by planning the next day. When I get up in the morning, I know exactly what I'm going to do that day—which projects I will be working on, who I have to talk to, which goals I have to reach.

As I go through my day, I maintain a careful balance between keeping my commitment to my plan and remaining flexible as conditions change throughout the day. I don't let anything distract me from my goals—yet there are always emergencies and unexpected events that arise and have to be dealt with. It's important to stay focused and to keep moving forward—but not so focused that you can't respond to the needs of your spouse, your children, your friends, or your neighbors as those needs arise.

When I get to work, I work. I run through my "Things to Do" list and I get a lot of satisfaction from checking off item after item. When it's time to take a break for lunch, I eat a light, healthy meal. When it's time to exercise, I go out and work up a sweat. I come back feeling energized to get more work done.

There are times, of course, when my energy level sags, my enthusiasm wanes, and I just don't feel like working! We all feel that way sometimes. Well, that's okay. Take a break, do something else and don't feel guilty. But make it a short break and then get right back to work and keep being productive. Push through the laziness and sluggishness, and soon the old pep and enthusiasm will return.

Remind yourself of your commitment to use God's gift of time wisely and productively. Keep a jar of marbles on your desk. Write motivational sayings on three-by-five-inch cards and post them around your office. Do whatever it takes to stay enthused and energized. Treat each Sacred Now as a holy and irreplaceable opportunity to achieve your dreams and fulfill your purpose.

At the end of the day, make plans for the next day. Think about how much fun it's going to be to tackle this project or confront that challenge. And when you ease your head onto your pillow that night, thank God for the gift of another day, well invested.

Forget the Past

In May 2004, my daughter Karyn and I ran the Disney Marathon together in Orlando. Before the start of the race, she shared a quotation with me that had made a big impact on her life: "Though no one can go back and make a brand-new start, anyone can start from now and make a brand-new ending." Those words put a lift in every step of the next 42.2 kilometers.

Life is a marathon, and sometimes there are steep hills, moments of utter exhaustion and discouragement, experiences of heartbreak and a sense that the whole world is passing you by—but in life, as in a marathon, you can also start where you are and make a new ending. As someone once said, it's never too late to be what you might have been.

You may think, "But I'm too old to be what I might have been! My life has already passed me by!" Don't you believe it, my friend. When I ran in the 2003 New York Marathon, one of my fellow marathoners was a ninety-two-year-old man of Indian ethnicity who lived in London. I ran alongside him for a while through the streets of Brooklyn, and though his stride was not quick, it was strong. He was an inspiration to me, and he taught me that attitude, more than age, determines what we can accomplish in life.

Sir Francis Chichester was sixty-four when he sailed around the world, completely alone, in a fifty-three-foot yacht. Sir Winston Churchill was sixty-five when he became prime minister of England and led that nation's heroic struggle against Nazi tyranny. Golda Meier became prime minister of Israel at age seventy-one.

Ronald Reagan was sixty-nine when elected to his first term as president of the United States, vowing to restore a foundering economy and topple Soviet communism; he was seventy-seven years and 349 days old when he left office at the end of his second term. By that time, the economy was booming and communism was crumbling; the Berlin Wall fell just ten months after he left office—just as he had predicted.

Michelangelo was sixty-six years old when he completed the ceiling of the Sistine Chapel; he was eighty-eight when he painted the frescoes in the Pauline Chapel. Architect Frank Lloyd Wright completed his masterpiece, the Guggenheim Museum, when he was eighty-nine. Celebrated folk artist Grandma Moses began painting in her seventies and had her first one-woman exhibit when she was eighty.

Former president George H. W. Bush went skydiving on his eightieth birthday. When asked why, he replied, "I was yelling at Father Time, 'Take that, you old man!'" And fitness expert Jack LaLanne stated at age eighty-nine, "Any stupid donkey can die. Dying is easy. Living's a pain in the backside. You've got to work at it!"

Benjamin Franklin was seventy-eight when he invented the bifocal lens and eighty-one when he signed the U.S. Constitution. Ben Franklin's life teaches us that you are never too old to achieve—yet his life also teaches us that you are never too young, either. At age twenty-three, he owned and operated his own newspaper, *The Pennsylvania Gazette*. He founded the first public library at the age of twenty-five. In Philadelphia at age thirty, he started the nation's first fire department. At thirty-seven, he invented the first heat-efficient stove, the famous Franklin stove.

So don't tell me you're too old *or* too young. You are just the right age to seize the opportunity of this very moment, this Sacred Now.

Don't waste a moment of your life regretting past failures or yesterday's lost opportunities. All that matters is today. New Zealand's famed short story writer, Katherine Mansfield, once said, "Regret is an appalling waste of energy; you can't build on it; it's only for wallowing in." And poet Henry Wadsworth Longfellow reminds us, "Look not mournfully into the past. It comes not back again. Wisely improve the present. It is thine. Go forth to meet the shadowy future without fear."

Joe Torre, legendary manager of the Yankees, compares life to baseball. "During my eight years as a player with the Braves," he said, "I was fortunate to hit behind baseball's all-time home run king, Hank Aaron. One day, Hank and I were talking about batting slumps, when he made a comment that's stayed with me ever since: 'Each at-bat is a new day.' . . . In baseball, a hitter mired in a slump can belt a home run on any pitch. A team on a prolonged losing streak can always win that day's game. In business and life, the best way to overcome a pattern of failure or loss is to re-focus on 'today.'"

It's true. In order to start where you are, you've got to forget past failures—and, I've found, you also have to forget past glories.

One of the sweetest memories of my NBA career was the 1982–83 season when I was general manager of the Philadelphia 76ers. The fans and sportswriters had been predicting an NBA championship for

Philadelphia ever since we brought Julius Erving to the team in 1976, yet that gold ring proved elusive in the first six years of Dr. J's tenure with the team. Finally, in 1982–83, everything came together. We swept the Knicks, four games to zip, in the Eastern Conference semifinals, then beat Milwaukee four games out of five in the Eastern Conference finals, and then we swept Kareem and the Lakers to win it all.

The triumphant Sixers returned to Philly for a hero's welcome. The team rode on flatbed trucks through the heart of the business district, down South Broad Street, all the way to Veterans Stadium. Along the way, the players were showered with confetti and cheers of adoration from an estimated one million fans. For a week after that celebration, I walked six inches above the ground.

The treasured memento I received of that championship season was a diamond-studded gold ring with the inscription "Defense and Persevere," the team's motto. It was so big, it was like wearing a solid gold electric toaster on my knuckle! Whenever I was working at my desk or talking on the phone, that ring riveted my gaze. I found myself staring at it, watching it sparkle, thinking back to that incredible season—

And I realized I wasn't getting anything done. I was so fascinated with that ring and the glories of the past that I wasn't focused on the season ahead of us. I finally realized that those past glories were undermining my ability to live in the present and seize the opportunities of the Now. So I reluctantly put that ring back in the box and slipped it into a drawer. It's been more than twenty years now, and I haven't taken that ring out of the box more than two or three times.

I found out that the old saying is true: "If what you did yesterday still looks big to you, then you haven't done much today." The apostle Paul expressed it this way: "Forgetting what is behind and straining toward what is ahead, I press on toward the goal to win the prize for which God has called me heavenward in Christ Jesus" (Phil. 3:13–14).

C. S. Lewis observed in *The Screwtape Letters* that "the Present is the point at which time touches eternity." That is so true! When we truly seize this present moment, this present opportunity, and we offer it up in service to God, we use our time to affect our eternal destiny—and we truly do touch eternity.

So don't hesitate. Don't procrastinate. Start where you are. Start right here.

And start right *now*.

The Power of One

by Jay Strack

On February 7, 1996, Randall White, Kevin Farr and Brian Hernandez, all eighteen, spent the evening bowling just outside of Tampa, Florida. A little before midnight, they got into their Chevy Camaro and went for a drive east of town. As they drove through the intersection of Lithia-Pinecrest and Keysville roads, their car was broadsided by an eight-ton truck. All three were killed instantly.

These young men had not been drinking or speeding. They had not been negligent in any other way. Why did the accident happen? Because someone had uprooted the stop sign that normally guarded that intersection.

Three young pranksters, all about the same age as the young men who died, had gone around the Tampa area, taking down stop signs—just to see what would happen. The perpetrators—two boys and a girl—were convicted, though a state appeals court later tossed out their convictions because of prosecutorial errors.

Imagine what would happen if all the stop signs and traffic lights in our society were suddenly removed one night. What kind of chaos would result? How many people would die? Who would want to live in a world without stop signs?

Yet that is precisely the kind of society Shamgar lived in. It was a civilization without stop signs, without order, without justice. Twice in the book of Judges—in Judges 17:6 and 21:25—we read this bleak description of the days in which Shamgar lived: "In those days there was no king in Israel, but every man did that which was right in his own eyes."

There was no king in Israel—no law, no justice, no standard of right and wrong. And yet, in some ways, here we are, 3,000 years later, and it can still be said that people do that which is right in their own eyes. We live in a postmodern world—a world in which the old rules have been torn down and the old values have been uprooted.

Though the general public is largely unaware of postmodernism and how it has changed their world, postmodern thinking now dominates the news media, the entertainment media, the legal establishment and the education establishment. In place of traditional morality, postmodernism gives us moral relativism. In a postmodern world, there are no rules, no ultimate truths—and no stop signs.

We have removed all the signs that determine the rules we should all play by. Our entire culture lives by the slogan of Outback Steakhouse: "No rules, just right." Just do whatever feels right for you. So, despite the fact that we are separated from Shamgar by half a world and thirty centuries, we have something in common with him. Like Shamgar, we live in times when moral and social standards have broken down, when people do that which is right in their own eyes.

So our world needs men and women like Shamgar, people who are willing to step into the moral vacuum and do what is right and righteous. The history of ancient Israel, as recorded in the Old Testament, is the history of a nation that sank into moral and spiritual chaos, accompanied by social breakdown and desolation. Could America be headed for the same destination?

I don't know the answer to that—but I do know that these are times that cry out for people to take a stand where they are, to use what they have, and to do what they can. Proverbs 14:12 tells us, "There is a way that seems right to a man, but in the end it leads to death." We live in a culture where everyone follows a way that seems right, but which leads to death because it leads away from God.

It was not uncommon, during the time of Shamgar, for the people to worship the pagan gods of the surrounding culture instead of the one true God of Israel. They would turn to Moloch, the brass fire-god to whom children were horribly sacrificed, or to Baal, the sun-god of the Canaanites. By turning to alien gods, the people of ancient Israel removed themselves from the guidance and protection of the God who had delivered their forefathers from slavery in Egypt.

I am reminded of a crime that was committed in May 2003—a theft of an artwork from the Museum of Fine Arts in Buenos Aires, Argentina. The stolen piece was a small sculpture called "La Main de Dieu" or "The Hand of God." It was sculpted by the French master Auguste Rodin in 1898 and depicts a hand molding a small human form. It symbolically portrays how God's hand shapes and fashions our lives. The day after the theft, the newspaper headlines in Buenos Aires shouted, "The Hand of God is Missing!" People were asking each other, "Where is 'The Hand of God'"?

That was the crisis that afflicted Israel in the days of Shamgar. Because people had fallen away from acknowledging God in their lives, because "every man did that which was right in his own eyes," the hand of God was missing from Israel. No one could find the hand of God.

So Shamgar stepped into the moral vacuum and accepted the challenge of saving his nation from the invading hordes of Philistine terrorists. He started where he was, out on his farm, and sized up the situation—then he used what he had and did what he could.

Seize the Opportunity

In 2 Timothy 4:2, the apostle Paul issues this challenge: "Be prepared in season and out of season." I like the way this is expressed in the old King James Version: "Be instant in season, out of season." Be instant! Be ready right now, instantly! To be instant is to be focused, to have our eyes on the goal at all times, regardless of whether the conditions around us are favorable or unfavorable. Be instantly ready and prepared to seize every opportunity, to meet every challenge, to respond to every threat.

To be instant, in the original Greek language that Paul uses, literally means "to be steady, ready, and at hand." The mental picture Paul suggests with these words is that of a soldier with his hand resting on the hilt of his sword. His sword isn't drawn yet—but he's ready, he's instant, he's prepared to respond to changing conditions and unexpected events. Paul is calling us to be ready and prepared to give our all to any opportunity that presents itself, whether in times of great prosperity or times of harsh adversity.

One phrase Paul uses—"in season, out of season"—is more significant than it seems at first glance. The Greek word that is translated "season" is actually derived from the Greek word for "opportunity." It is the same word that is used in Luke 4:13, in the story of Satan's temptation of Jesus in the wilderness. In the King James Version, this verse tells us, "And when the devil had ended all the temptation, he departed from him for a season"—or, as the New International Version (NIV) puts it, "When the devil had finished all this tempting, he left him until an opportune time." So when Paul says that we should be "instant in season, out of season," he is telling us to be always ready and alert to those opportune moments that come our way.

The apostle Paul didn't just preach—he practiced what he preached. Do you know where he was when he wrote those words, "Be instant in season, out of season"? He was in chains, locked up in a Roman prison. For years, God had used Paul in mighty ways. The apostle had preached and founded churches throughout the entire region around the eastern Mediterranean Sea. He had debated the great philosophers of Athens. He had met with Peter and James and helped to shape the future of the church for centuries to come. He had written immortal treatises on theology and Christian living, such as his letters to the Romans, Corinthians and Thessalonians.

But suddenly those busy days were over. He could do nothing but sit and pray and write letters from a stone-walled cell. He was a prisoner of Nero and the Roman Empire.

Here was a man who had once appeared to be the league MVP of the Christian church—God's most valuable player. Suddenly, he was reduced to MVB—most valuable benchwarmer. Paul was a doer, a mover and a shaker, so it must have been terribly frustrating to be unable to do, move or shake anything.

Yet, even in prison, Paul made a choice to start where he was, use what he had and do what he could. While he was in prison, he wrote some of his most famous and most powerful letters—Colossians, Philemon, Ephesians, Philippians, and, near the very end of his life, 2 Timothy. Those letters are, in places, poignant and painful to read. Again and again in those letters, we read such lines as, "Remember my chains," and, "I am an ambassador in chains. Pray that I may declare [the Gospel] fearlessly, as I should," and, "What has happened to me has really served to advance the gospel."

Paul was willing to go wherever God sent him, even to prison. He was willing to start there and to be instant in season and out of season.

He was prepared to do God's work and spread the Gospel whether his opportunities were great and plentiful ("in season") or meager and few ("out of season").

Opportunity has been defined as a "wind that blows favorably." The Greek word for opportunity suggests the image of a great ship with its sails billowing at full mast, the ship clipping along at top speed toward its destination. The word suggests dynamic momentum. So if we are instant and alert to the opportunities that come our way, we will be like ships that have their sails unfurled and ready to catch the favorable winds of opportunity.

Tragically, most people in this world are like ships at anchor, with their sails furled and secured, their masts bare, dead in the water. The winds of opportunity blow past and the ships continue to sit at anchor, going nowhere, their hulls collecting barnacles. By contrast, Shamgar was a ship that was going places, a ship that was simply unstoppable.

The Greek sculptor Lysippus lived four centuries before Christ and is credited with more than 1,500 statues and artistic works. Renowned for the delicacy of detail in his statues, Lysippus is considered one of the first sculptors to focus on the detailed rendering of hair in his subjects. Lysippus worked in bronze and modeled his statues after heroes, athletes and the Greek gods. He was also the portrait sculptor of Alexander the Great.

My favorite work by Lysippus is his male statue of Opportunity. With careful detail, Lysippus carved a powerfully symbolic image of Opportunity. It is the image of a powerfully built man with wings on his feet and a huge lock of hair on his forehead. Seen from the back, however, the man's head is bald. What do these symbols mean?

The winged feet mean that Opportunity is moving swiftly and won't be here for long. The lock of hair on Opportunity's forehead is something to grab onto and hold, to keep Opportunity from slipping away. But the baldness of the back of Opportunity's head tells us that, once it has passed you by, there is nothing you can take hold of. If you let Opportunity go, it may never be within your reach again.

Shamgar clearly understood the powerful truths illustrated by this statue of Lysippus. He knew that opportunities must be grabbed as soon as they come within reach or they will be lost. He looked around him and saw that the roads and highways of his nation were deserted, his neighbors were cowering in fear and bands of terrorists were coming into his country. It was a time of crisis—and a time of opportunity. In Shamgar's mind, opportunity was not just knocking, it was kicking down the door!

My friend Pat Williams can tell you all about the thrill of watching one of his players seize an opportunity to make a clutch shot in an NBA game—and about the crushing disappointment when a player lets that opportunity slip by. Games and even entire championships have been decided because a player either took or passed up an opportunity that lasted as briefly as two or three-tenths of a second. An instant of hesitation can cost you a game and subject you to years of regret.

In your own everyday life, you may have only minutes, seconds or even a fraction of a second to:

- turn the wheel and slam on the brakes in time to save precious lives.
- make the most important decision of your career.
- speak a word of hope to someone who is considering suicide.
- introduce yourself to the person who could become the love of your life.
- say "I love you" to someone you may never see again.

• share the message of God's grace and forgiveness with a lost and
hurting soul.

A brief hesitation could carry a big price tag. An opportunity, once
lost, may never come again. Napoleon is reported to have said, "There
is, in the midst of every great battle, a ten- or fifteen-minute period
that is the crucial point. Seize that period of time and you will win the
battle. Lose it—and you will be defeated." So be alert, be instant, be
prepared. Seize the opportunity when it comes.

Do you believe in the reality of Satan? I do! And I believe our adver-
sary, Satan, would like nothing better than to dull our senses and make
us lazy and inattentive so that he can steal away our opportunities. This
is the satanic strategy for neutralizing us and hindering us from reaching our full potential for the Kingdom of God.

In *The Screwtape Letters,* C. S. Lewis depicts a senior devil named
Screwtape who writes letters of advice to a junior devil, his nephew
Wormwood. This junior devil is trying to neutralize a young Christian,
so Screwtape offers this satanic advice: "The great thing is to prevent
his doing anything. As long as he does not convert it into action, it does
not matter how much he thinks about this new repentance. Let the
little brute wallow in it. . . . Let him do anything but act. No amount of
piety in his imagination and affections will harm us if we can keep it
out of his will."

So we must convert our beliefs into action. Let's start where we are
and make the most of every opportunity to do great things for God.
Whether we work in an office or in the home, whether we are in prison
like Paul or in a field behind a pair of oxen like Shamgar, let's start
where we are and make an impact on our world.

The Gulag Opportunity

If there is one person of our times who can identify with the apostle Paul, it would be the Russian novelist and historian, Alexander Solzhenitsyn. On February 8, 1945, Solzhenitsyn was sentenced without a trial to eight years of hard labor in the gulags—the Soviet forced labor camps that were used primarily to imprison political dissidents. His crime: Solzhenitsyn had criticized Soviet dictator Joseph Stalin in a private letter to a school friend (the Soviets censored everything in those days, including the mail). At the time of his arrest, Solzhenitsyn was a committed Marxist and had served with distinction in World War II as an artillery captain in the Soviet army. None of that mattered to the judge who sentenced him to hard labor.

In 1950, Solzhenitsyn was sent to a prison camp in Kazakhstan, where he developed a cancerous tumor. He was operated on by doctors at the camp hospital, then moved to a surgical ward. As Solzhenitsyn lay in his cot, feeling hot, feverish and too weak to move, a doctor sat down beside him. Solzhenitsyn knew the doctor slightly. His name was Boris Kornfeld, and he was a gentle, soft-spoken man who wanted someone to talk to.

It was dark, and the ward was deserted except for Solzhenitsyn and Dr. Kornfeld. As Solzhenitsyn listened, the doctor talked about his life. It seems that Dr. Kornfeld had once served as personal physician to Stalin. After Kornfeld had given years of faithful service to him, the dictator turned on Kornfeld, had him arrested and sent him to the gulag.

While Kornfeld was in prison, he came to believe in Jesus Christ as his Lord and Savior. Solzhenitsyn later recalled feeling "astonished at the conviction of the new convert, at the ardor of his words." Dr. Kornfeld talked about his past sins and how he deserved nothing but punishment—yet God had sent Jesus to die in his place and save him from his sins. Solzhenitsyn would later say that he sensed "such mystical knowledge" in Kornfeld's voice that he trembled in his cot.

After Dr. Kornfeld had finished his story, he got up and went into the next room, lay down on a cot and went to sleep. Awhile later, Solzhenitsyn also drifted off to sleep.

Solzhenitsyn was awakened at dawn by voices and the sound of footsteps in the corridor. Hospital orderlies were carrying Dr. Kornfeld's limp body to the operating room. Sometime during the night, someone had crept into the hospital and hammered his skull with a mallet as he slept. Dr. Kornfeld died on the operating table, having never regained consciousness.

Solzhenitsyn was profoundly affected by the fact that the last words the doctor had ever spoken were the words he had said at Solzhenitsyn's bedside—the story of his life-changing encounter with Jesus Christ. Dr. Kornfeld's words would continue to haunt Solzhenitsyn over the next few months.

The surgery had been unsuccessful, and Solzhenitsyn's condition worsened. In 1953, he was sent to a cancer clinic in Tashkent, where he received radiation treatment and was cured. He later told biographer Joseph Pearce (author of *Solzhenitsyn: A Soul in Exile*) that after being stricken with cancer, then cleansed of it, "I came back to a deep awareness of God and a deep understanding of life." He believed that God had spared his life for a purpose, so he committed his life to Jesus Christ.

Soon after his release from prison, Solzhenitsyn published several works that revealed the dehumanizing conditions faced by political dissidents in the Soviet Union, and particularly in the labor camps.

Those works included *One Day in the Life of Ivan Denisovich, Cancer Ward,* and *The First Circle*—novels that were banned in the USSR, but hand-copied and widely distributed throughout the literary underground. The KGB (the Soviet intelligence and internal security agency) tried to suppress his writings, but his work garnered so much worldwide acclaim—including the Nobel Prize for literature in 1970—that the Soviet authorities were afraid to move against him.

Though he would have been welcomed abroad, Solzhenitsyn chose to remain in Russia, hoping he could play a part in reforming the totalitarian Soviet government. In 1974, however, Solzhenitsyn published a powerful nonfiction work, *The Gulag Archipelago,* which bluntly detailed the Soviet Union's extensive use of terror and torture against its own citizens. After that book was published, Solzhenitsyn was arrested, stripped of his citizenship and deported.

For twenty years, he lived in exile in Switzerland and the United States. His writings—especially *The Gulag Archipelago*—are credited as being one of several factors that directly led to the collapse of Soviet communism in 1991.

After the fall of the Soviet Union, Solzhenitsyn returned to Russia where he spoke out on the deepest needs of the Russian people. Their need, Solzhenitsyn said, is not political or economic. It is spiritual. The Russian people, he said in his last public appearance in Moscow, had lost "the ability to answer the principal problem of life and death. People are prepared to stuff their heads with anything, and to talk of any subject, but only to block off the contemplation of this subject." The only solution to the problem of life and death is finding eternal life through Jesus Christ.

Looking ahead to his own death, Solzhenitsyn said that it would "be just a peaceful transition. As a Christian, I believe there is life after death."

Like Shamgar and the apostle Paul, Solzhenitsyn is a man who started where he was—prison. He used what he had—his memories of his sufferings and his ability to write about them with power and clarity. He did what he could—at great personal risk, he told his story to the world. And the world was impacted and changed by his story.

Think Cumulatively

You might wonder how Shamgar even knew that Israel was being invaded. After all, he had no CNN or Fox News Channel to tune in to. He had no newspaper. He was out in the hinterland, living the rustic life of a Palestinian farmer. We don't know for sure, but it's possible that Shamgar farmed the uplands of southern Palestine, the same area where an immensely rich man named Abraham had once owned a vast cattle ranch. From that high, hilly land, Shamgar could probably look out over the plains, all the way to the sea. He may well have watched the Philistines raid the land of Israel on many occasions, from either land or sea.

The Philistines commonly used terrorist-style attacks—small-scale strikes rather than massive invasions. By the time the Israelites could assemble and mobilize a fighting force to launch a counterattack, the Philistines would be gone, only to return later in a different place.

Watching these invasions from a distance, hearing the stories of how his neighbors were being attacked, robbed and slaughtered, Shamgar became outraged over the violence of the Philistines. But what could he do? Though he was only one man, he couldn't stand idly by as the Philistines burned the fields of his neighbors and plundered his nation. The Philistines had invaded his land one time too many—enough was enough!

When Shamgar decided to attack the Philistines, he had no assurance that his mission would succeed. He knew that the odds were against him, and that he was likely to fail and die in the attempt. But Shamgar was a leader. He did what leaders do: he made a decision to act, regardless of the personal cost, regardless of the chances of success.

Shamgar also demonstrated an important principle of leadership: You can't be a leader tomorrow if you are not a leader today. It is useless to say, "At some time in the future, I'm going to impact the world. Tomorrow, I'm going to make a difference." Authentic leaders start where they are. They understand the simple (but often neglected) truth that you can't start where you aren't. You have to start where you are.

You can't impact the world by wishing you were something you are not. If you are a student, a pastor, an insurance salesman or a farmer, you probably are not in a position to change the foreign policy of the United States of America. But even if you are not the president or the secretary of state, you can still impact your world.

If you are a student, you can have an influence on the students and teachers at your school. If you are a pastor, you can have a profound influence on the lives of your parishioners. If you are an insurance salesman, you can help your clients make wise, important decisions for the benefit of their families. And if you are a farmer, like Shamgar, then start at the farm! Grab your ox-goad or your John Deere tractor, and do what you can!

Being a farmer, Shamgar understood the principle of multiplication: start with one plant and soon you have more. If you plant one kernel of wheat in the ground, it will grow up to produce a stalk bearing up to three heads of wheat. In each head are from fifteen to thirty-five kernels of wheat. So one kernel of wheat can easily produce more than a hundred new kernels of wheat at harvesttime. Plant those hundred kernels and they can produce a hundred times a hundred kernels, or ten thousand. Those ten thousand kernels can yield a million new kernels, and on and on and on!

But remember, it all starts with a single kernel of wheat. It all starts with the power of one.

You must start where you are, even if you are just one little person in the world, even if you think there's nothing one person can do. I call this "cumulative thinking." If you will begin to think cumulatively, if you will start where you are, use what you have and do what you can, there is no limit to what God can accomplish through you. There is no limit to the power of one.

Today, many people believe that human society pretty much runs on autopilot, steered and driven by forces that are beyond the influence of any individual human being. Yet as we look at human history, we see that individual people—people just like you and me, people who were willing to start right where they are—have often had a profound effect on the course of human events.

In 1962, a government scientist named Rachel Carson published a book called *Silent Spring*, which showed in clear, scientific terms how the pesticide DDT enters the food chain and becomes deposited in the fat tissue of animals and human beings, causing cancer and genetic damage. Though DDT had been a valuable tool for eradicating malaria-carrying insects across the world (and had won its inventor a Nobel Prize), Rachel Carson was virtually the only person in the world who had studied the dangers of this pesticide to human beings.

When her book was published, a firestorm of controversy erupted. Yet her facts and conclusions were so carefully documented that it quickly became clear that the world should heed her warning. One example of the positive effect that *Silent Spring* had on our nation:

there were more than 500,000 bald eagles in America when that majestic creature was selected as our national bird in 1872; by 1963, only 417 breeding pairs were known to exist. Though there were a number of factors contributing to the eagles' decline, their numbers had been decimated, in large part, by DDT poisoning.

Rachel Carson's book was largely responsible for the creation of the Environmental Protection Agency under President Nixon. Use of DDT was banned in the United States in 1973, and the environment dramatically rebounded from the damage it had suffered. In 1999, the bald eagle, which had been nearing extinction, was removed from the list of endangered species.

Change begins when one person says, "I will start where I am, use what I have and do what I can." That's the power of one. That's the power of cumulative thinking.

Ronald Reagan was just one man, but he believed in the power of one. Even before he ran for president, he told friends and associates his simple plan for dealing with the Soviet Union. He planned to abandon the "détente" approach of previous presidents (endless rounds of diplomatic concessions, cultural contacts and economic talks) in favor of a strategy he described in four words: "We win, they lose."

When Reagan's own foreign policy advisors heard his plan, they were aghast. They feared he would lead the nation into war. After all, American prestige and power were in decline, and the Soviets were advancing, having solidified their hold on Eastern Europe, taken over Afghanistan, and established client states in Central and South America, right on America's doorstep. Most American foreign policy experts feared the USSR and urged Reagan to moderate his rhetoric, to make concessions, to avoid angering the Russian bear.

Ignoring the timid advice of the diplomats, Reagan pursued his "We win, they lose" strategy for eight years. At the beginning, he was just one man with a vision for toppling the "evil empire" of the Soviet Union. But Ronald Reagan was a cumulative thinker. He started where he was, a lone opponent of Soviet expansionism, and soon he was joining forces with others who had the same vision of a world without an Iron Curtain: Pope John Paul II, Czech dissident Vaclav Havel, British prime minister Margaret Thatcher, Polish Solidarity leader Lech Walesa, and yes, Alexander Solzhenitsyn.

On June 12, 1987, Reagan went to Berlin's Brandenburg Gate and spoke those words that shook the foundations of the Soviet empire: "General Secretary Gorbachev, if you seek peace, if you seek prosperity for the Soviet Union and Eastern Europe, if you seek liberalization, come here to this gate! Mr. Gorbachev, open this gate! Mr. Gorbachev, tear down this wall!"

The Berlin Wall was opened by East Germans on November 9, 1989, and torn down by the end of 1990. On December 26, 1991, the Supreme Soviet officially dissolved the USSR, and the Soviet Union passed into history, just as Ronald Reagan had predicted it would before he even ran for president: "We win, they lose." That's the power of one. That's the power of cumulative thinking.

Clara McBride Hale was an African American woman who was born in 1905. Her father was lynched by a white mob when she was nine years old; her mother died of natural causes when she was sixteen. When she was in her early twenties, her young husband, Thomas Hale, was diagnosed with cancer; he died two weeks later. While her grief was still fresh, Clara Hale—a widow with two children—decided she would channel her grief into doing good for others. In 1940, she opened a home for needy children, offering both foster care for orphans and inexpensive day care for working mothers. Over the years, she became known as "Mother Hale."

In the late 1960s, Mother Hale was thinking about retiring. She had rescued and raised dozens of kids. But then a woman came by Mother Hale's home, holding a baby. She seemed dazed, and Mother Hale believed she was addicted to drugs. That day, Mother Hale decided she couldn't retire yet. Instead, she founded a new ministry to children who were born addicted to the drugs their mothers abused.

With the help of local politicians, Mother Hale moved her home for at-risk babies to a large brownstone building in Harlem. With that, the organization called Hale House was born. "Before I knew it," she later said, "every pregnant addict in Harlem knew about the 'crazy lady' who would give her baby a home."

In the 1980s, as the AIDS crisis exploded in our cities, Mother Hale responded by taking in children of AIDS-infected parents or children born with HIV, the virus that causes AIDS. Before most people in America had even heard of AIDS, Mother Hale was fighting the disease on her own doorstep. In 1985, President Ronald Reagan honored her by inviting her to stand and be recognized during his State of the Union Address. "Harlem and all of New York needs a local hero," he said. "Mother Hale, you are the one. . . . Anything is possible in America if we have the faith, the will and the heart."

"I love children and I love caring for them," she once said. "That is what the Lord meant for me to do." Mother Hale died in 1992 at age eighty-seven, but her work goes on. Hale House continues to serve children who are abandoned, neglected, sick or drug-addicted. That's the power of one. That's the power of cumulative thinking. Mother Hale started where she was in her Harlem apartment, she used what she had, she did what she could, and thousands of babies were rescued as a result.

You don't have to be rich or powerful or famous to make a positive impact on your world. You just need to bloom where you're planted. You just need to start where you are. That's all anyone can do.

And it's always enough.

The Second Secret:
Use What You
Have

The Tale of Shamgar: Part Two

S hamgar summoned two dozen of his nearest neighbors for a meeting at the home of Giddel the Potter. The men gathered in a circle, crouching on their haunches or sitting cross-legged in the shade of the spreading fig tree next to Giddel's house.

"And who were these men who slew our brother Reuel and his family?" asked Tobiah, a stout, white-maned man in his sixties. He and his sons tended a vineyard near the river.

"They were Philistines," Shamgar said, then he spat on the ground, a sign of contempt for their godless enemy.

The other men murmured. "Philistines!" said one of them. "Are you sure?"

Shamgar stood, took something from the pouch on his belt and tossed the thing on the ground in the center of the circle. The others drew back as if from a scorpion.

It was the amulet of Dagon the fish-god that had hung around the neck of the Philistine commander. There was a grim silence.

"They wore armor and carried swords," Shamgar said at last. He crouched down so that he could look each man in the eye. "It was not just a band of robbers that I slew. They were soldiers of Philistia."

"These are troubled times," said Asaph the Carpenter. "We have abandoned the roads and villages because of outlaws in the land. But at least the nation has been at peace. No armies of other nations have dared to invade Israel since Ehud, the last judge over Israel, defeated King Eglon of Moab eighty years ago."

"The days of peace are gone," Shamgar said. "The enemy has come against us from the south, from the plains of Philistia, from Ashkelon, Ashdod and Gaza. I killed a dozen of them, but more will come."

"More have already come," said one of the older men. "I arose before dawn and went up to the Rock of Tefillah to pray and I saw armored men moving through the olive grove below. I counted more than fifty of them. I hid myself and watched them pass. Their speech was strange. I didn't know then, but I know it now: they were Philistines."

"What can we do?" asked Tobiah. "Israel has no king, no army!"

"I have shown you what we can do," said Shamgar, clenching his fist around his ox-goad, which was stained with Philistine blood. "We must fight. We must drive the Philistines out of our land."

"My sons and I are vinedressers, not soldiers," said Tobiah with a dismissive gesture. "We cannot fight the Philistines."

"Am I not a farmer?" said Shamgar. "Am I not a man of the soil like you, Tobiah? Like most of the men here? I drive oxen and push a plow. But when the Philistines butchered my friend, I became a soldier and I killed a dozen men."

"Where are these Philistines you killed?" asked one of the younger men. There was a tone of skepticism in his voice, as if he did not believe that one farmer could kill a dozen armed outlanders.

"I piled the bodies beside the road, near the Oak of Adin," Shamgar said. "I left them there for the carrion birds to feed on. Their bones will serve as a warning to any other Philistines who pass by."

"Fool!" Tobiah snapped angrily. "Your 'warning' will only anger the enemy! You should have hidden the bodies!"

Shamgar spat on the ground. "These uncircumcised Philistines have invaded your nation and slain your neighbors," he said hotly, "and you worry about making them angry? Are we men of Israel? Or are we sheep, handing ourselves over to be slaughtered? If we do not fight, if we do not drive them out, they will do to us what they did to Reuel and his family. They will slaughter and rape and leave our land desolate!"

"But we can't fight them," said Tobiah. "There are no swords in Israel. The art of forging swords has been lost in eighty years of peace."

Shamgar sighed, then turned to Giddel the Potter. "Giddel," he said, "you told me your father served alongside Ehud against the Moabites. Where is his sword?"

"I still have it," Giddel said. "It's hidden in my house."

"Bring it out," Shamgar said, rising to his feet.

Giddel went into his house, then returned with a sword laid across his outstretched hands. He looked shamefaced—and Shamgar soon saw why. The iron blade was nicked and rusty. The edge was worn and dull. Shamgar reached out and grasped the ancient weapon by the haft. The blade rattled where it was fitted into the haft. Shamgar turned the sword upside down, and the blade separated from the haft and clanged on the hard ground.

"That," Shamgar said bitterly, "is what our nation has become."

There was a long, embarrassed silence.

"If only Joshua were alive today," said Dishon the Harodite. "He would know what we should do. We would all follow a man like Joshua."

Shamgar crouched and eyed the other men. "Joshua would tell you just what I have told you," he said. "He would tell you to fight. If you would fight alongside Joshua of old, then will you not fight at my side?" Shamgar swept the circle with his gaze, but no man would meet his eye.

"Perhaps we could make peace with the Philistines," offered Tophel, an old man whose speech whistled because he had no teeth. "Perhaps if we taxed our people and gave the money to the Philistines, they would leave us in peace."

This set off another round of murmuring. Several men thought Tophel had a good idea. Only two or three men offered even a weak disagreement.

"Enough talk!" Shamgar snarled, startling the other men. He rose to his feet, gripping his ox-goad. "Who'll come with me? Will just one of you stand at my side and fight the Philistines?"

No one stood. No one moved. There was no sound but the buzzing of flies.

"Very well," Shamgar said in a voice that was gentle—and sad. "You are afraid, and I don't condemn you for it. The enemy is fierce and well-armed. You are not soldiers and you have no weapons. So I say to you: stay in your homes. If the Philistines come to your door, protect your families as well as you are able. Use whatever you have to kill as many as you can. And pray for me."

Shamgar turned and walked away from the men who sat under the fig tree.

"Wait!" shouted Tobiah. "You are just one man! What are you going to do?"

"What I can," Shamgar said without slowing his step.

What Is Your Ox-Goad?

by Pat Williams

What a difference thirty centuries make.

Shamgar's job would have been so easy if he could have faced all of those Philistines from the turret of an M1 Abrams battle tank or from the cockpit of a Blackhawk helicopter armed with 7.62 mm machine guns. But he didn't have that kind of firepower at his disposal.

All he had was an ox-goad. That's it. Just a long wooden pole.

Shamgar's resources were limited, to say the least. But he took his limited resources and offered them fully to God. He used what he had.

Why didn't Shamgar have a sword, shield or helmet? Because he wasn't a professional soldier. He was a man of the soil, not a man of war. So when the Philistines swarmed into Israel and stalked his land, Shamgar had to face them with nothing in his fist but a long sharpened stick. In the hands of Shamgar, however, that spindly stick became as lethal as a Tomahawk cruise missile.

Shamgar was the third in a series of judges whom God raised up to lead the nation of Israel during the years between the death of Joshua and the rise of King Saul. The judges of Israel were not formally recognized leaders. They were not elected, appointed, anointed or installed. Israel had no formal leadership whatsoever. "In those days," the book of Judges tells us, "there was no king in Israel, but every man did that which was right in his own eyes."

And what the people thought was right in their own eyes was horribly wrong in the eyes of God. The people fell away from God and his Law. They began worshipping the demon-gods of the surrounding culture. Their society began to crumble and decay, and in time they were taken captive by neighboring nations. While in captivity, the people would repent and return to God, and God would raise up a new leader, a judge, a person who had enormous natural leadership abilities. That judge would then deliver the people from their bondage.

The first of these judges was Othniel, who victoriously led an army of Israelites against the Mesopotamians. The second judge was Ehud, whose army killed 10,000 soldiers of Moab. But Shamgar, the third judge, is very different from Othniel and Ehud. He does not lead an army. He is an army of one. He faces a hopeless situation—and he faces it alone and friendless.

Why was Shamgar alone? Perhaps it was because he couldn't get anyone to join him. I suspect that the nation had sunk into such moral decline that there simply wasn't a man within miles with the courage to stand with Shamgar and guard his back.

Then again, it's possible that Shamgar simply preferred to work alone. He may have decided that none of his neighbors had the stealth, the strength, the courage and the physical prowess to fight a vastly superior enemy like the Philistines. He may have decided that his chances were better if he acted alone than if he relied on the dubious "help" of his neighbors. Whatever the reason, we know that Shamgar fought alone, armed only with an ox-goad.

Why an ox-goad? Certainly there must have been a better weapon available than a pointed wooden pole!

Actually, an ox-goad may have been the closest thing to a weapon that anyone in Israel had anymore. The nation had probably fallen into such a state of moral and social decline that the arts of the weapon-smith and the blacksmith had been lost. It may well be that no one in Israel knew how to make a proper weapon anymore.

There were, after all, similar times in Israel's history. For example, about four centuries after Shamgar, in the early days of King Saul, identical conditions prevailed. The book of 1 Samuel records:

> *Not a blacksmith could be found in the whole land of Israel, because the Philistines had said, "Otherwise the Hebrews will make swords or spears!" So all Israel went down to the Philistines to have their plow-shares, mattocks, axes and sickles sharpened. The price was two thirds of a shekel for sharpening plowshares and mattocks, and a third of a shekel for sharpening forks and axes and for repointing goads. So on the day of the battle not a soldier with Saul and Jonathan had a sword or spear in his hand; only Saul and his son Jonathan had them.* 1 Samuel 13:19–22

Imagine a nation that had sunk so low that it had to trade with its enemies in order to arm itself for battle! Such a nation places itself at the mercy of its enemies and puts itself at serious risk of extinction.

That appears to have been the condition of Israel in the days of Shamgar. The people had such a complete lack of national pride and self-respect that they had abdicated their duty to defend themselves, their families, and their land against foreign invaders. Throughout the land of Israel, not a sword or a shield could be found, not even a spear or a dagger. The closest thing in the whole country to a weapon of any kind was a farmer's ox-goad.

The impression we get of those times was that Israel consisted of a vast Silent Majority. The people all knew that the Philistines were invading their land, killing and robbing and raping their people, so they said, "Somebody ought to do something about this! Somebody ought to call out the army, call out the Marines! Why doesn't somebody do something?" There was no one in the entire country who would say, "I'll step up, I'll take responsibility." No one would say that—

Except Shamgar.

Seven Resources

Did the people look up to Shamgar as a leader? No. He was just a farmer like the rest of them. I don't believe Shamgar was recognized as a hero and a judge over Israel until *after* he had achieved his amazing victory over the Philistines.

So the Philistine terrorists roamed Israel, killing entire families, taking what they wanted, operating without opposition. The situation was so bad, we are told, that "the roads were abandoned; travelers took to winding paths" (Judg. 5:6). The people abandoned the roads and the villages. They huddled in fear out in the wilderness, just praying that their enemies wouldn't find them. In all of Israel, only Shamgar dared to take up an ox-goad and make a bold stand at the bloody crossroad of history.

Shamgar started where he was and he used what he had. He picked up his ox-goad and went to war.

You may say, "But my resources are so limited that I can't even afford an ox-goad! I'm willing to start where I am—but with what? I literally don't have anything at all to take into battle!"

My friend, you have more resources than you can even begin to imagine. Even if you don't have a sharp stick, you have a powerful arsenal of resources at your disposal. Offer those resources to God and you will be absolutely amazed at what he chooses to accomplish through you.

If you are willing to start where you are, use what you have and do what you can, then you can become a hero like Shamgar. But if you refuse to use the resources God has given you, then you are no better off than Shamgar's cowardly neighbors, who huddled in the wilderness, afraid of the open roads, scared of their own shadows.

So what is your ox-goad? What do you have to work with?

I want to suggest to you seven possessions that God has given you— seven powerful resources that you can use to become a person of action like Shamgar. I'm sure you have many, many more resources than the ones I am about to list, but I have no doubt that you at least have these seven.

These are your ox-goads. After I have listed them for you, pick them up and get going! Start where you are, use what you have and do what you can with the resources God has given you.

1. Your Dreams

You have your dreams. You might say, "Dreams! Is that all? What are dreams good for? What can I do with dreams?"

My friend, every great accomplishment began as a dream. The automobile, the airplane and the space shuttle all had their beginnings in the human imagination. Neil Armstrong's footsteps on the moon were the fulfillment of decades of dreams—the dreams of science fiction writers and engineers and an American president, John F. Kennedy, who was assassinated before he could see the dream come true.

America itself was a dream in the minds of the Pilgrims and the Jamestown colonists, the revolutionaries and the founding fathers. Millions of Americans of all races have freedom and equality and opportunities that their parents and grandparents never dreamed of—and why? Because Dr. Martin Luther King, Jr., had a dream, and he dared to make that dream come true.

Shamgar dreamed of liberating his people from the terrorism and oppression of the Philistines. Then he took up his ox-goad and made that dream a reality. So what are your dreams? Have you taken the time to look beyond what is, and to envision what could be?

Dreams are incredibly powerful. They fill us with hope. They enable us to imagine a better tomorrow. They motivate us and energize us. They activate our courage so that we will dare to take risks in order to see our dreams come true.

Our dreams should be bold, audacious, even a bit scary. Pastor Andy Stanley, senior pastor of North Point Ministries, Inc., in Atlanta, and author of *Visioneering*, keeps a card on his desk that reads, "Dream no small dreams, for they stir not the hearts of men." Dream big dreams, then dare to do whatever it takes to hammer those dreams into reality.

The former center of the Orlando Magic, Zaza Pachulia (now with the Milwaukee Bucks), was born in Tbilisi, Georgia, in the former Soviet Union. He played professional basketball in Turkey (Euroleague) before entering the NBA draft in 2003. His mother, Marina, was a big basketball fan, and Zaza caught basketball fever from his mom when he was nine years old. He literally papered the walls of his bedroom with pictures of Michael Jordan.

Marina would use basketball to motivate Zaza to work and study hard. If his school grades slipped, she would hide his basketball and his shoes until his grades improved. At night, Marina would tuck Zaza into bed and tell him a bedtime story: "Once upon a time, there was a boy who grew up to play basketball in the NBA. The crowds cheered him in every big city across the U.S.A., because he made every shot and he scooped up every rebound."

Every day and every night, Zaza dreamed of playing basketball. Today, Zaza Pachulia is living his hardwood dreams. "All I ever dreamed about is the NBA," he once said, "and now I am here."

Dreams are a powerful, life-changing resource. Don't ever say you have no resources to accomplish great things. Everyone has the power to dream, and dreaming is the first step to achieving. The bigger your dream, the greater your accomplishment.

People will tell you, "Don't be such a dreamer! Be practical!" Half of the people who tell you that mean well—they don't want you to be disappointed when you fall short of your dreams. The other half are envious of your dreams; they're afraid you'll succeed and they won't. Whether they mean well or not, those who try to squash your dreams are not doing you any favors. Don't listen to them. Just keep on dreaming.

Let me tell you something about you that you may not even be aware of, but it's absolutely true: you were born for greatness! I mean that with all my heart. You may say, "But Pat, you don't even know me! How can you say I was born for greatness?" Answer: because we were all born for greatness. We were all created in the image and likeness of God, and God designed us to do great things.

I'm not saying you were necessarily born to be rich or famous or to alter the fate of nations. But true greatness rarely has anything to do with such things. The truly great people in this world are the ones who dream of making a difference in lives, even if it's only a few lives. Great people will take the time to make a difference in the lives of needy children, or people in a retirement home, or veterans in a VA hospital, or people who are trapped in poverty or addiction or shut up behind prison walls.

Anyone can be great, because anyone can reach out and make a difference in the lives of other people. So dream great dreams, as God intended you to. Then make those dreams come true and become the person God made you to be. Shamgar had a dream and an ox-goad, and he saved his people. What is your big dream?

2. Your Enthusiasm

John Marcus Templeton once defined enthusiasm as "that state of exuberance in which all things seem possible." Even overcoming six-hundred-to-one odds? Absolutely! I don't believe Shamgar could have done what he did without enthusiasm, without that wild-eyed belief that, through the power of God, all things were possible.

Enthusiasm is energy. It electrifies the soul. Plug into the power of enthusiasm and you'll be amazed at what you will accomplish. The poet Ralph Waldo Emerson once put it this way: "Every great and commanding movement in the annals of the world is a triumph of enthusiasm."

You might say, "But I don't have any enthusiasm." To which I would reply, "Why not? If you believe in God, you should be overflowing with enthusiasm!" After all, the word enthusiasm comes from the Greek word *entheos*, which means, "in God." If you are "in God" and if God is in you, then your life should be brimming with enthusiasm, energy and inspiration.

Beethoven always believed that when he was composing music, he was in tune with his Creator. On one occasion, he introduced one of his newly written symphonies to an orchestra. In the middle of the rehearsal, one of the violinists stood up and complained, "This section is so difficult and awkward that it is simply unplayable!"

Beethoven glared at the violinist. "When I composed that passage," he said, "I was inspired by Almighty God, the Maker of the universe! Do you think I can consider your puny little fiddle when God speaks through me?"

That's enthusiasm talking! That is a man filled with *entheos!* As someone once said, "Enthusiasm is faith set on fire." If you truly have faith in God, you can't help having enthusiasm. If you truly have something to be enthusiastic about, then you have a reason for living.

Former Milwaukee Bucks all-star forward Marques Johnson put it this way: "It's the sport that I love, not the business. The business end messes everything up. I almost wish there was no money in it. Then we could all go out and enjoy playing like we did when we were kids. I'd still play if there was no money, because it's the best game there is, and you can play all the time if you want. Anybody who's ever been into it, pro or playground, knows what I'm talking about. When I'm playing ball, it's like I'm not even part of the Earth. It's like I belong to a different universe." That's enthusiasm! That's *entheos!*

Enthusiasm makes your mind sharper, your arm stronger, and your feet swifter. Enthusiasm lifts your spirits and fires up your will to persevere. Enthusiasm motivates and empowers you. Enthusiasm can often compensate for a lack of money, skill or talent. A plan that might otherwise fail often succeeds on the strength of enthusiasm alone.

If you lack enthusiasm, then pray for it. Ask God to fill up your soul with a passionate enthusiasm to do his will and to accomplish the great life's mission he has given you. The Bible is filled with enthusiastic expressions of praise to God and confidence in his ability to do anything through us, even the seemingly "impossible." Here are just a few examples:

Shout with joy to God, all the earth! Sing the glory of his name; make his praise glorious! Psalm 66:1–2

My lips will shout for joy when I sing praise to you—I, whom you have redeemed. Psalm 71:23

Everything is possible for him who believes. Mark 9:23b

I can do everything through him who gives me strength. Philippians 4:13

That is the enthusiasm and confidence that comes with authentic faith in God. If we believe in God, it should show on our faces, it should turbocharge our voices, it should fill us with a confidence that literally everything is possible because we are possessed by *entheos.* God is in us!

Writer Maurice Boyd tells of the time conductor Eugene Ormandy dislocated his shoulder while conducting a symphony by Brahms. In the margin of the score, Brahms had written at one point, "As loud as possible!" Then, a few measures later, he wrote, "Louder still!" It was at that point that Ormandy conducted so vigorously, athletically and enthusiastically that he threw his shoulder out of joint.

"I know some people who have reached middle age," Boyd concluded, "and have never had an enthusiasm great enough to dislodge a necktie, let alone their shoulder."

What about you? What is the one thing in life that fills you with a joint-straining, body-spraining enthusiasm? Writer Diane Ackerman once expressed a conviction that should be your life's goal and mine: "I don't want to get to the end of my life and find that I lived just the length of it. I want to have lived the width of it as well."

Andy Russell was a legendary Steelers linebacker—the gap-toothed, roaring leader of Pittsburgh's "Steel Curtain Defense." Russell once recalled how he learned the true depth of enthusiasm from defensive tackle Ernie Stautner.

> *Ernie comes into the huddle and his thumb is broken back against his wrist. There's a tear near the break and his bone's sticking out. He has a compound fracture of the thumb. He takes his thumb in his hand and he wrenches it down into his fist. Doesn't show it to anybody. Doesn't say anything. Looks up and says, "What's the defense?"*
>
> *I thought to myself, "I'm not in the right business!"*
>
> *So, he stayed there for the rest of that series and then we came off the field. I'm watching him because I'm the only guy who saw that he had a compound fracture. I saw the bone. So, I'm figuring now he's going to ask for a doctor, and he may have to go to the hospital, because this thing could get infected.*
>
> *But he says, "Give me some tape." So they throw him some tape, and he just starts taping this huge ball. He makes this big fist; then, we go back in. He plays the entire game, never misses a down. I'm just astounded and he's using this hand, which is broken, as a club. He's beating people with it.*
>
> *After the game, we go into the locker room and he says, "Hey, Doc, I think I got a problem," and I'm thinking, "This is just unbelievable!" That is passion for what you do. That guy was making no money. He just loved to play.*

That's the power of enthusiasm. It can make you indomitable, undefeatable, even when your body is broken and wracked with pain. Enthusiasm can lift you above adversity and give you the winning edge.

3. Your Talent

"If we did all the things we are capable of doing, we would literally astonish ourselves." So said the astonishing Thomas Alva Edison, the

Wizard of Menlo Park, the inventor of nearly 1,400 patented inventions. It's true. We are capable of so much more than we dream or imagine. If we would simply start using even 10 percent of the talent and ability we have, we would probably be amazed at how much we could accomplish.

It has been said that amateurs built Noah's Ark; professionals built the *Titanic*. Great achievements are often produced by people of relatively modest talent who are willing to offer it all to God for the service of others. Shamgar was a farmer, not a warrior, yet he offered whatever talents he had to God, and God used him to save a nation.

Don Shula, the winningest coach in NFL history, once said this about players with talent: "Coaches have a tendency to stay too long with people with 'potential.' Try to avoid those players and go with a proven attitude. Players who live on 'potential' are coach-killers. As soon as you find out who the coach-killers are on your team, the better off you are. Go with the guys who have less talent, but more dedication, more singleness of purpose."

If you tell me, "I can't accomplish anything, I don't have any talent," I want you to know that you have all the talent you need. The only thing you lack is a willingness to use the talents you have! You may not have the entrepreneurial ability of Bill Gates, the writing ability of James Michener, the artistic ability of Picasso, the athletic ability of Michael Jordan or the preaching ability of Billy Graham, but so what? You have all the ability you need to carry out the mission God has given you—if you will put 100 percent of your ability to use for God.

Billy Sunday, the great preacher of the early twentieth century, said, "More people fail through lack of purpose than through lack of talent." What most of us need is not more talent, but the willingness to do more with the talent we have. Don't worry about being the best. Just make the best of the talents you have.

Composer Igor Stravinsky was once approached by a film producer to write a movie score. Stravinsky listened as the producer described the script and told him who would star in the film—but when the producer mentioned the fee, Stravinsky jumped to his feet. "Four thousand dollars!" he said. "You expect me to score an entire film for four thousand dollars!"

The producer told Stravinsky that another famous composer had recently completed a picture for the very same amount.

"But there's no comparison!" Stravinsky countered. "He's a much more talented composer than I am! I have very little talent, so for me the work is much more difficult and will take me much longer to complete. I could not accept the assignment for anything less than eight thousand dollars."

The producer met Stravinsky's price.

You may think you have very little talent—but you have enough talent for any challenge you face. Your responsibility is to make the most of the talent you have, to start where you are, and to use what you have.

4. Your Education

Melville Weston Fuller was chief justice of the U.S. Supreme Court over a century ago. He was also very much involved in his church. Once, while he chaired a church conference, one of the conference speakers got up and spoke for half an hour on the evil influence of higher education. The man actually gave thanks to God that his mind had never been "polluted" by the wicked teachings of a university.

Fuller listened to this man until he could stand no more. He rose to his feet and interrupted the speaker. "Am I to understand, sir," Fuller said, "that you are giving thanks to God for the blessings of ignorance?"

The man looked a little confused, then replied, "Well, yes, I suppose I am."

"In that case," Fuller said, "you have much to be thankful for."

I don't know how much education Shamgar had. He probably had little formal schooling—but he clearly had enough education to complete the mission God gave him. His education may have consisted of hearing the stories of Israel's heroes—Abraham, Isaac, Jacob, Joseph, Moses and Joshua. Perhaps he learned military tactics by sitting around a campfire and listening to his father, Anath, recount the stories of Joshua's battles at Hazor and Jericho. Perhaps he learned stealth and guerilla tactics from the account of Joshua and Caleb's spy mission in the land of Canaan.

What kind of education do you have? An MBA or a PhD? A bachelor's degree in arts or science? A high school diploma? Or a head full of street smarts from the School of Hard Knocks? Whatever your level of education, that is a resource you can use to achieve your life goals and to fulfill your God-given mission in life.

Albert Einstein, who gave us the theory of relativity, once said, "Education is that which remains when you have forgotten everything you learned in school." That's so true! Most of us think that education is something you pour into an empty skull during four or more years at a university. In reality, the purpose of a university is not to *complete* the process of education but to ignite a lifelong love affair with learning.

As the late billionaire publisher Malcolm Forbes said, "The purpose of education is to replace an empty mind with an open mind." In other words, to be educated does not merely mean that you have learned what you need to know. It means that you know how to learn, how to unlearn, and how to relearn. The world is changing too quickly to allow your knowledge level to remain static. Changes in society, the economy and technology are taking place so rapidly that what was true this morning may no longer be true this afternoon.

According to Hamilton Securities of Washington, D.C., if we represented the population of the entire world as a village of 100 people, it would look like this: There would be 14 North and South Americans, 21 Europeans, 8 Africans and 57 Asians. Fully 70 of those 100 people would be nonwhite and an equal number would be non-Christian. Half of the world's wealth would be in the hands of 6 people. No fewer than 80 of those 100 people would live in substandard housing, 70 would be illiterate and 50 would suffer from malnutrition. And here's one final statistic that should change the way you look at your life: *Only one of those 100 people would have a college education.*

What about you? Do you have a college education? If you do, you have a resource in your hand that 99 percent of the people in this world do not have. What are you doing with that resource? That diploma of yours is your ox-goad. It's time to start where you are, use what you have and do what you can with that educated mind of yours.

5. Your Experience

Dr. John MacArthur is the pastor of Grace Community Church in Sun Valley, California. As a twenty-one-year-old college football player, he was honored with a trophy at an awards banquet. He got up to speak, and in the course of his short acceptance speech, he talked about his love for Jesus Christ.

After the banquet, a man came to him and said, "There's a girl in the hospital who really needs your help. She's really depressed and needs to hear what you said tonight about Jesus Christ."

"I'm not a pastor or a counselor," MacArthur said.

"You don't have to be," the man said. "Just tell her what you told everyone tonight. You don't have to preach. Just tell her your story."

So MacArthur went to the hospital. The girl in the hospital bed was an attractive high school cheerleader named Polly. She was depressed because her boyfriend had accidentally shot her in the neck, severing her spinal cord. Polly was paralyzed for life.

Young John MacArthur haltingly introduced himself, then said, "I can't imagine what you are going through."

"If I had a way to do it, I'd kill myself," Polly replied bitterly. "I don't have any reason to live."

MacArthur didn't know what else to say, so he started telling the same story he had told at the awards banquet—the story of how he had given his life to Jesus Christ. He wasn't sure if Polly was even listening, but he kept talking.

Finally, he said, "You know, it's not what happens to your body that matters. It's what happens to your eternal soul. I know it's hard for you to understand this now, but I'm sure that God can bring joy into your heart, even after all that you are going through. But first you have to decide where you will spend eternity. Would you like to hear how you can know that you will spend eternity in heaven with Christ?"

"Sure," she said. "Tell me. I'm desperate."

So the young football player told Polly that Jesus had nailed her sins to the cross so that she could be forgiven and cleansed. When he had finished, he said, "Polly, would you like to commit your life to Jesus Christ and receive him as your Lord and Savior?"

"Yes," she whispered. "I would."

So they prayed together. For months afterward, John would return to the hospital and visit Polly. She had up days and down days, but she was clearly changed. The bitterness and suicidal depression were things of the past. On one visit, she said, "In some ways, John, I'm glad this happened to me. If it hadn't, I wouldn't know Jesus."

John MacArthur kept in touch with Polly, and in time she met and married a Christian man who loved her regardless of her disability. But not only was Polly's life changed by this experience—so was MacArthur's. The experience of being used by God in this way completely changed the way he viewed his own life. He said to himself, "Running around on a field with a football under my arm means nothing. Touching lives with the love of Jesus Christ—that's what matters. Reaching others with the power of the Gospel is all I want for my life. Nothing else even comes close."

This experience was the turning point that led John MacArthur into ministry. What are the experiences that God wants to use in your life?

No matter what other resources we think we lack, we can't deny that we have experience. Every day we spend on this planet is one more day of experience. Our experiences may not all be triumphs and successes, but so what? Failure is usually a far better teacher than success—if we are willing to learn the lessons. As former Houston Astros pitcher and manager Larry Dierker observed, "Experience is the best teacher, but a hard grader. She gives the test first, the lesson later."

Isn't *that* the truth! Sometimes it seems that experience is a thing that we don't get until after we need it! But if we approach our lives with a positive and teachable attitude, we will learn the lessons of our experiences in time for the next big test.

We should always remember that experience is not what happens in our lives, but *how we respond* to what happens in our lives. The poet Archibald McLeish once said, "There is only one thing more painful than learning from experience and that is *not* learning from experience." A great deal depends on our attitude toward our mistakes: It is much more helpful and useful to think of them as "experiences" rather than "failures." The word "failure" suggests "The End," but the word "experience" conveys the idea of a detour on the road to success.

I have given a lot of thought to how Shamgar could have gained the military experience to single-handedly destroy a force of six hundred Philistine warriors, armed only with an ox-goad. The answer kept coming back to me: he couldn't have had *any* military experience. Not only did Israel have no king and no army, but the nation had not had a war in eighty years.

So I asked myself: What kind of experience did he have? Answer: He must have been an experienced *hunter*.

Think about it: The oxen on his farm were for pulling a plow, not for making ox burgers or oxtail soup. He probably raised wheat on his farm, which was a staple in the diet of Middle Eastern people 3,000 years ago. What, then, did Shamgar do for meat? Most likely, he hunted. What did he hunt with? He had no bow and arrow, or he would have used such a weapon against the Philistines. So he must have hunted with his ox-goad, using it as a club or a spear.

So when the Philistines invaded Israel, what did he do? He did what he had always done. He did what his experience had taught him to do. He hunted. He picked up his ox-goad and used it the same way he had used it to hunt bears, mountain lions and deer. Only this time, he hunted Philistines.

He started where he was, he used what he had—his ox-goad and his experience as a hunter—and he did what he could. That is a powerful lesson for your life and mine.

With every experience in life, whether good or bad, pleasant or painful, we should ask ourselves, "How can I put that experience to good use? What can I learn from that? What is the lesson I can apply to my life, my career, my ministry, my relationships?" All the things that happen to us—a breakdown on the freeway, getting fired from a job, serving on a jury, going through bankruptcy—are experiences that can increase our character and wisdom. But we only grow from them if we actively, prayerfully look for the lessons that are embedded in those experiences.

The French philosopher and novelist Albert Camus wisely said, "You cannot create experience. You must undergo it." In other words, we cannot manufacture our experiences. We cannot always choose what we will experience. Life comes to us whether we are ready or not. Our job is to undergo our experiences, accept them, learn from them and recognize that everything we go through is part of God's grand plan to mold us and shape our character.

6. Your Influence

David Blankenhorn, founder of the Institute for American Values and author of *Fatherless America,* tells the story of a man who entered a barbershop and began talking to a teenage boy who was sweeping the floor. As they talked, the man realized that the boy had no father. "Son," he asked, "who would you want to be like when you grow up?"

"Mister," the boy said with an edge of bitterness in his voice, "I ain't never met nobody I want to be like when I grow up."

Those words break my heart.

Young people need heroes and role models. They need people who will *influence* them to become all that they are capable of becoming. We all have the gift of influence. We influence others through our words, our example, our caring, and our actions. In fact, we can't help but influence others. The only choice we have is whether our influence is for good or ill.

People are watching us all the time, even when we don't realize it. They notice when our talk and our walk don't match. They can spot hypocrisy in an instant. So if you want to be a person of influence, then be a hero and a role model to the people around you.

Actress and country music star Reba McEntire once put it this way: "Our kids need heroes. Our kids need somebody to look up to. And y'all are it." She's right. Look at the children and teenagers around you, in your home, your neighborhood, your church. They are looking for people of character and integrity, people to pattern their lives after. They need heroes—and y'all are it.

My life has been shaped by my heroes and mentors. One of those heroes was Andy Seminick—the famed Phillies catcher of the late 1940s and early '50s. When I was a boy, Andy was my idol. Fact is, he's one of the reasons I wanted to be a catcher when I got into college and professional baseball.

I had gotten to know Andy while I was a teenager, hanging around Shibe Park in Philadelphia. He was one of the Whiz Kids, the National League pennant-winning Phillies of 1950. In 1962, when I started playing pro baseball with the Miami Marlins of the Florida State League, the manager of the club was none other than Andy Seminick, my boyhood hero.

I spent two years playing for Andy, and he had an enormous influence on my life. One of the values Andy drilled into us was tenacity: "You've got to be tough," he often said, "and you've got to play hurt." You want to know what kind of influence Andy Seminick had on me? I'll tell you.

In January 1997, thirty-five years after I had first played for Andy, I played in a Phillies/Cardinals Dream Week game in St. Petersburg, Florida—what they call "an old-timers' game." I was behind the plate, catching at age fifty-six. Larry Andersen, the former major league reliever, was pitching.

Larry threw a hard slider, and I caught it right on the thumb of my catching hand. I felt a bolt of electric pain, and I saw that the top joint of my left thumb was completely knocked out of the socket. I ran over to the dugout and called for the trainer, who pulled on the joint and popped it back into place. That thumb was still throbbing—but I ran back to the plate and continued catching.

Why did I keep playing? Because Andy Seminick, my boyhood idol and first pro manager, was on the bench in the dugout. Even though he was seventy-six years old by that time, and I was fifty-six, I could still hear his voice in my brain, saying, "You've got to be tough, and you've got to play hurt." So I went back in the game and played hurt for Andy.

Now, *that* is influence!

My greatest hero is Jesus of Nazareth, a man who had more lasting influence on the world than any other human being in history. He spent three intense years pouring his life into twelve men. Though he preached to the masses, he concentrated his influence in the lives of a few individuals. He deeply and profoundly influenced twelve men, and through them, he changed the world.

Jesus practiced his influence on others by being an example and a role model. When he wanted to teach his disciples about prayer, he didn't say, "You ought to get on your knees and say these words." He took them out into the olive grove and he prayed with them all night long. When he wanted to teach them what it means to serve others, he didn't say, "Here's what you need to do." He got down on his knees, took a basin and towel, washed their feet and set an example for them to follow. That's influence.

Jesus didn't just say, "Listen to me." He said, "Follow me. Learn from my example. Do as I do." If we want to have an influence on the people around us, then we need to become heroes and role models. We need to get down in the trenches with people and pour our lives into their lives.

When I think of Shamgar, I wonder what kind of influence he had with his friends and neighbors. He was probably respected as a local businessman, a farmer, a man who grew the grain that helped feed his community. But I suspect that when he went to his neighbors with a plan to drive the Philistines out of their land, his influence reached its limit.

I can picture Shamgar calling his neighbors together to discuss the Philistine problem. I can imagine him telling his friends, "We have to band together and drive these Philistines out of our land! If we work together, we can defeat them! Now, every man who's with me, step forward!" And I can see all of Shamgar's trembling neighbors taking three steps back!

"Look, Shamgar," one of them might have said, "you're a fine wheat farmer and a real asset to our community. But let's face it—you're no Joshua! There isn't one true military genius in all of Israel. We all just want to hold on and keep our families hidden until the Philistines get tired of killing us and decide to go home. If you want to attack them, go ahead—but you'll have to attack them alone."

So Shamgar did exactly that! After single-handedly wiping out a force of six hundred Philistines, his influence expanded enormously! From then on, Shamgar was recognized as a judge over all of Israel—and a person of national influence.

Our influence must be used responsibly. Hall of Fame baseball manager Sparky Anderson put it bluntly:

> *Athletes who say they ain't role models for our youth are dumber than Bozo. They don't deserve a dime of their millions. They're totally missing the boat. God gave them all this special ability, and then they take the*

money and snub their noses at the kids or anybody who happens to be in their way. They've got to understand that they have the chance to be a leader. They can teach our young people by the way they live their lives.

Whether they like it or not, every athlete is a role model. So is every adult. Our children look up to us. Every day, we get the chance to influence more young lives than we can ever imagine. Sometimes, it just takes a smile or a pat on the shoulder. Maybe all it takes is a couple of minutes to listen to a youngster's problems. I believe that if an athlete does something dumb, like getting hooked on drugs or alcohol, he should then be penalized double. That's the price for abusing the precious gift they've been given.

As I write these words, the Orlando Magic organization has drafted and signed Dwight Howard, an eighteen-year-old, 6'11" forward straight out of high school, as the number one pick in the 2004 NBA draft. Dwight has set the basketball world on its ear, not only because of his amazing skills on the court, but because he is a young man who takes his position of influence seriously.

Dwight's dad, Dwight, Sr., is a state trooper and the athletic director at Dwight's former school, Southwest Atlanta Christian Academy. His mother, Sheryl, is a P.E. instructor at the school. The Howards raised their son with strong Christian values, attending church several times a week. Right up to the day he left home for Orlando, Dwight was required to do his chores, clean his room, and keep his curfew.

What kind of guy is Dwight Howard? His language is squeaky clean. He likes rap music, but he's selective—no music that demeans women or glorifies drugs and violence. His favorite movie is Disney's G-rated *Finding Nemo.*

While a student at Southwest Academy, a K–12 private Christian school, Dwight used his influence as a basketball star to be an encourager and a positive role model to the younger kids. In the hall-ways or on the playing field, he would talk to the grade-schoolers about what they were learning in school, or he'd give them a few basketball pointers. His teachers all speak highly of his attitude, char-acter, and commitment to his schoolwork.

Everyone who knows Dwight is impressed by his strong, outspoken faith in Jesus Christ. When Dwight signs autographs, he adds the phrase "God Bless!" to each signature. Though he received a number of glitzy, expensive gifts upon graduating, his favorite gift, was a mod-estly priced Bible to replace the one he lost at school.

He says that basketball is his platform, given to him by God to enable him to share his faith with others. Even so, he doesn't want to shove his beliefs down anyone's throat. "People think I'm trying to go in and get on the podium and make everybody a Christian," he says. "That's not my goal. My goal is to let my actions speak louder than my words."

In other words, he intends to live his life as an influence for God.

When he was only in the ninth grade, Dwight wrote out his life goals. Topping the list: "Be the first draft pick in the NBA." He achieved that goal and has now set an even more ambitious goal: He wants to change the image of the NBA from that of a league of arrogant bad boys to an image more resembling his own humble, church-going "choirboy" persona.

Some cynical sports commentators predict that Dwight's good-guy idealism will melt under the glare of NBA stardom. They say that the available young women, the drugs and alcohol, the pride, and all the other temptations that come with fame and wealth will prove too much for a young man from a "sheltered" existence. And I admit in all candor that I pray daily that God will strengthen and protect this bold young Christian. I believe that personified evil truly does exist in this world, and I am convinced that there is nothing Satan would love more than to get his hooks into Dwight Howard.

But I also know that if there is one young man who is well-armored and well-equipped for the battle ahead, a young man committed to using his influence for God, that young man is Dwight Howard.

To be a person of influence, you don't have to be a basketball star. You don't have to be a person of great status and station in life. No matter who you are and what you do, you can be a person of influence. You have the opportunity to impact the lives of many people every day—family, friends, neighbors, coworkers, young people, old people and even the people you meet in the shops and offices where you do business.

What kind of influence are you having on the lives around you? How are you using the God-given resource of your influence on others?

7. Your Wisdom

Another resource that most of us have (but are quick to overlook) is our wisdom. I'm not talking about intelligence, knowledge or education. There are many people who are not particularly well educated but are amazingly wise. And there are also people who could achieve a perfect score on the Mensa test, yet who are utterly bankrupt in the wisdom department. As someone once said, "Never mistake knowledge for wisdom. One helps you make a living; the other helps you make a life."

When I was young, I was very impressed by people who were smart or talented or gifted in some way. As I've grown older, I've become much more impressed by people who are wise—people who have a deep understanding of life and who can explain how to live effectively for God and for others. Where does wisdom come from? The Bible tells us,

"If any of you lacks wisdom, he should ask God, who gives generously to all without finding fault, and it will be given to him" (James 1:5).

National Security Advisor Condoleezza Rice is a devout Christian and a woman of prayer. Once, when she was asked what she prays for, she said, "I was taught that you don't pray with a laundry list. So, I ask for wisdom and guidance and strength of conviction."

We gain wisdom as we cooperate with God while he seeks to shape and mold our lives. Wisdom doesn't come to us all at once—*wham!*—like a bolt of lightning. It is built up gradually within us as we learn and grow from the many experiences that life sends our way. We become wiser as we become more patient, tolerant, caring, compassionate, loving, understanding and insightful. We become wiser as we learn to trust God more completely through the tests and trials of life.

The most important use of wisdom is in making good decisions. As Bible teacher Charles Swindoll once said, "Since wisdom is God's specialty, it's imperative that we seek his wisdom prior to every major decision." The wiser we become, the more we are able to see life from God's perspective—and the easier it becomes to make good decisions in difficult circumstances.

No question, as Shamgar faced the great crisis of his life—the invasion of his homeland by the Philistines—he needed more than his trusty ox-goad at his side. He needed wisdom. He needed help from God in making a tough decision: Should he go out alone, braving impossible odds, to fight the enemy? Or should he pack up his family and his belongings and seek safety until the Philistines had left? I have no doubt that Shamgar spent long hours on his knees before God, seeking divine wisdom for a painfully difficult decision.

In the end, wisdom told Shamgar to stay and fight. He had no guarantee that he would win. But he had to start where he was, use what he had, and do what he could. So he mustered up his courage, his skill, and his wisdom—then with ox-goad in hand, he fought.

Dietrich Bonhoeffer was a man who faced a Shamgar-like decision. He was a pastor and theologian in the German Lutheran church in the 1930s. He watched with horror and disgust as the Nazi Party took over his nation—and as his fellow German churchmen began siding with the Nazis. In 1933, even before Hitler came to power, Bonhoeffer spoke out in a series of radio broadcasts in which he called for the German people to reject the Nazis and defend the rights of the Jewish minority.

By 1935, Bonhoeffer had become a leader in the Confessing Church, a wing of the Lutheran church that remained faithful to the gospel of Christian love and peace and that struggled against the increasing Nazification of German Christianity. He established an underground seminary that taught not only the Bible and theology, but the principles of nonviolent resistance. In 1937, the Nazi secret police (the Gestapo) closed the seminary and jailed many of the ministers of the Confessing Church.

In 1939, American theologian Reinhold Niebuhr helped secure a position for Bonhoeffer at Union Theological Seminary in New York. But after only three weeks in the United States, Bonhoeffer decided to return to Germany to suffer with his people. "I have had time to think and to pray about my situation," he said in a public statement. "I have come to the conclusion that I have made a mistake in coming to America. I shall have no right to participate in the reconstruction of the Christian life in Germany after the war if I did not share in the trials of this time with my people."

In 1941, Bonhoeffer joined Operation 7, an underground resistance and rescue movement that helped Jews escape to safety in Switzerland. By 1942, his involvement in the resistance took a fateful turn: Bonhoeffer joined a plot to assassinate Hitler.

The decision to take part in the death of another human being was a difficult one for Dietrich Bonhoeffer. He spent uncounted hours on his knees, imploring God for wisdom. Bonhoeffer was a pastor, a man of the Gospel, a committed pacifist. He had always taught his seminary students to seek a nonviolent solution to injustice. Murder was always wrong, he believed.

Yet he knew that the German state was committing mass murder on a scale unprecedented in human history. The fanatical hatred of one man, Adolf Hitler, was slaughtering millions of human beings. If he could help end the Nazi genocide by the assassination of Adolf Hitler, would it truly be murder? Or would it be an act of holy obedience, mercy and love? Though he prayed and prayed, Bonhoeffer could not decide whether killing Hitler would be right or wrong.

Despite his moral uncertainty, Bonhoeffer came to a practical, logical decision that it had to be done. As he told his sister-in-law, Emmi Bonhoeffer, "If I see a madman driving a car into a group of innocent bystanders, then I can't as a Christian simply wait for the catastrophe, then comfort the wounded and bury the dead. I must try to wrestle the steering wheel out of the hands of the driver."

So Bonhoeffer joined the conspiracy—a secret group that operated inside German Military Intelligence. Bonhoeffer's fellow conspirators included Admiral Wilhelm Canaris (head of Military Intelligence), General Hans Oster and Hans von Dohnanyi (the husband of Bonhoeffer's sister, Christine). Bonhoeffer acted as a courier, carrying messages to the Allies on behalf of the resistance.

During his involvement in the plot against Hitler, Bonhoeffer was living in a Benedictine monastery near Munich, working on a book entitled *Ethics*. When you read that book, you discover that he was actually searching his mind and soul for wisdom for making difficult moral decisions in a time of extreme crisis. Even while he was taking part in an attempted coup d'état, he was writing a book and seeking answers to the moral and spiritual questions that troubled his soul.

In April 1943, Bonhoeffer and several of his associates were arrested by the Gestapo for their involvement with Operation 7—but the Gestapo agents didn't know about his involvement in the plot against Hitler. The thirty-seven-year-old Bonhoeffer was taken to Tegel Prison in Berlin; also arrested were his brother-in-law and sister, Hans and Christine von Dohnanyi. Bonhoeffer spent the next two years in prison.

Meanwhile, several assassination attempts were aborted. Finally, on July 20, 1944, Colonel Claus von Stauffenberg carried a briefcase bomb into a conference attended by Hitler. The colonel placed the briefcase under the table next to Hitler, then left the room, supposedly to make a phone call. The bomb exploded, killing four of Hitler's top officers. Hitler himself, however, had gotten up from the table moments before the bomb exploded. He survived the blast with a badly injured right arm.

Admiral Canaris was arrested, along with others who had conspired against Hitler—but the Gestapo still knew nothing of Bonhoeffer's involvement in the plot. In February 1945, Bonhoeffer was moved to the Buchenwald concentration camp. Two months later, the Nazis discovered Bonhoeffer's name in the diary of Admiral Canaris. An enraged Adolf Hitler personally demanded the execution of Canaris, Bonhoeffer, the Dohnanyis and anyone else involved in the assassination attempt.

In April 1945, Bonhoeffer was moved to the prison at Flossenburg, where Canaris was also held. His execution was set for the morning of April 9. That morning, the prison doctor found Dietrich Bonhoeffer kneeling before God, praying with such intensity that he wasn't even aware of the doctor's presence.

A short time later, Bonhoeffer was led from his cell to a scaffold in the prison courtyard. He went calmly and quietly. On the scaffold, he again knelt to pray one last time. Then the rope was placed around his neck, the floor dropped from beneath his feet, and Dietrich Bonhoeffer went into the presence of his God.

The tragic irony of Bonhoeffer's death is that, less than three weeks after he was hanged, Hitler committed suicide in a Berlin bunker. Germany surrendered a week after Hitler's death. So, in one sense, it seems that Bonhoeffer died for nothing. The plot failed, and Hitler eventually died anyway. If Bonhoeffer had simply stayed out of the plot against Hitler, he could have lived. Instead, he died at the age of thirty-nine.

But in another sense, Bonhoeffer did what he had to do, just as Shamgar did. Neither Bonhoeffer nor Shamgar had any assurance that their missions would end in victory. Happily, Shamgar defeated the Philistines. Bonhoeffer's mission failed, and he lost his life.

Even so, both Bonhoeffer and Shamgar did the right thing. Acting in God's wisdom, they opposed evil. Each, in his own way, sought to preserve his people and save his nation. Here, then, are two great examples for us to follow. There is no guarantee that our plans will succeed. But success is not the important thing. The results are ultimately God's responsibility—and God measures success differently than we do. Our job is to simply start where we are, use what we have and do what we can.

So, my friend, it's time to take stock of your God-given resources. Ask yourself, "What do I have to complete my mission in life? What is my ox-goad?"

Once you have your ox-goad in hand, then leap into action!

The Creativity of Shamgar

by Jay Strack

During the first two days of the *Apollo 13* lunar mission, the space engineers at Mission Control called it the smoothest flight in the history of the space program. The mission seemed to refute the ancient superstition associated with the number 13. *Apollo 13* was, after all, the thirteenth flight NASA had scheduled for space exploration. Blastoff took place on the thirteenth minute after the thirteenth hour on April 11, 1970. That date, 4/11/70, had associations with the number 13, because 4 plus 1 plus 1 plus 7 plus 0 equals 13. NASA had even scheduled the lunar landing to fall on April 13.

Near the end of the second day of the mission, the CapCom (capsule communicator) in Houston radioed the spacecraft, "We're bored to tears down here." About nine hours after that comment, all boredom abruptly ended. That was when Mission Control directed astronaut Jack Swigert to stir the cryogenic tanks—the spherical tanks that contained a slush of supercold oxygen. The tanks had to be stirred periodically to keep the oxygen from stratifying. Unfortunately, no one was aware that the tanks had been damaged even before they were installed on the spacecraft, and that they had been fitted with the wrong thermostatic switches.

Soon after Swigert began stirring the tanks, the hull of the spacecraft rang like a bell that had been struck by a two-ton hammer. Though none of the astronauts knew it at the time, the spacecraft's number two oxygen tank had just exploded, causing a failure in the number one tank as well. Two of the ship's three fuel cells were also disabled, resulting in a severe power loss. The ship and its three-man crew were 200,000 miles from home and rapidly losing power, light, oxygen and water.

Swigert reported to Mission Control: "Houston, we've had a problem."

At first, the three astronauts—Commander James A. Lovell, Jr., lunar module pilot Fred W. Haise, Jr., and command module pilot John L. Swigert, Jr.—were only concerned with one question: Can we still go to the moon? Within minutes, however, it became clear that they faced a much bigger question: Will we make it home?

The crew only had one chance: shut down all systems to conserve power, then scramble into the lunar module, *Aquarius*, and use it as a lifeboat. *Aquarius* was equipped to sustain two men for two days during a lunar landing and return. For the crew to survive, it would have to support three men for four days. Neither the three astronauts in orbit nor the engineers in Houston knew how they would be able to do it, but somehow they'd have to. *Aquarius* was all they had.

They couldn't go back in time and undo the disaster. They had to start where they were, use what they had and do what they could. NASA engineers began by listing the problems that had to be solved, then they brainstormed all possible solutions. The first problem was the rising level of poisonous carbon dioxide and the low reserves of oxygen. The filters aboard *Aquarius* were not designed to handle the carbon dioxide output of three astronauts.

The engineers in Houston finally came up with a plan for makeshift carbon dioxide filters constructed from materials that the astronauts had on board—plastic bags, cardboard and tape. The astronauts completed construction of the filters just as the carbon dioxide in the spacecraft was reaching a critical level.

Meanwhile, power consumption was cut to the bone. Engineers in Houston carefully computed how much power was needed to get home versus how much power remained in the batteries. There was scarcely a single ampere-hour of juice to spare.

Water consumption was also severely restricted since it was used not only for drinking but for cooling critical mechanical systems. Each crewman was allowed six ounces of water per day, a fifth of normal intake. Before the end of the flight, all three men were severely dehydrated. The three men lost a total of 31.5 pounds during their flight.

Because the spacecraft had been headed for the moon at the time of the explosion, it was not in position for a return-to-earth trajectory. A new course had to be computed for *Apollo 13*—a course that would swing the craft around the moon and back toward Earth for the return trip home. Ordinarily, the course would be aligned by a device called the "alignment optical telescope," which would locate a navigational star. The spacecraft, however, was surrounded by a cloud of debris from the explosion, making the alignment telescope useless. Once again, the astronauts had to use what they had in order to do what they could. Since they lacked a distant star to steer by, they devised a plan to use the sun itself as a navigational star.

Starting where they were, using what they had, doing what they could, the crew of *Apollo 13* managed to reenter the earth's atmosphere at just the right angle. The crippled spacecraft splashed down in the South Pacific at 1:07 P.M. Eastern Standard Time on April 17. The crew was recovered by the helicopter carrier U.S.S. *Iwo Jima*. Both the space-craft crew and the Houston engineering team proved highly proficient in the three success secrets of Shamgar.

As is usually the case, it was enough.

Think Creatively!

If you want to be like Shamgar, you have to be flexible, you have to be imaginative, and you have to think creatively. It's a cliché, but it's true: you have to be able to "think outside the box." An outside-the-box thinker can turn plastic bags, cardboard and tape into a life support system for a spacecraft. An outside-the-box thinker can turn six-hundred-to-one odds into a fair fight. An outside-the-box thinker can turn a sharpened wooden pole into a lethal weapon.

Shamgar had nothing to fight with but an ox-goad—a long wooden pole tipped with an iron point at one end and a chisel at the other. That sharp tip gave it something of a spearlike character. According to schol-ars and archaeologists, Shamgar's ox-goad could have been as much as ten feet long, since it needed to reach the rump of an ox from behind a plow. That would make it an unwieldy weapon at best—but it was all Shamgar had.

This is a powerful lesson for us all. We don't need all of the latest gadgets and all the bells and whistles in order to do great things. All we need is what we have, plus the creativity and imagination that God has already given us.

God calls us to make a difference wherever we are, using the resources he has entrusted to us. Those resources might include material assets, such as money or technology or planes, trains and automobiles. But, as

Pat Williams showed in the previous chapter, those resources could also include such intangible resources as your dreams, enthusiasm, talent, education, experience, influence and wisdom.

Sometimes we focus so much on what we don't have that we fail to focus on what we do have! We don't have to be millionaires or sports stars or gifted public speakers or talented musicians to make a positive difference in the lives of people around us. All we need is the willingness to be as creative as we can with the resources we have. As the life of Shamgar shows, the biggest difference between success and failure is not so much our *resources* but our *resourcefulness*.

What is the talent God has given you? Is it a talent for leadership or making money? A talent for singing or drawing? A talent for building computers or running Web sites? A talent for teaching children or encouraging old people? A talent for serving tables and washing dishes? A talent for knitting afghans or crocheting pot holders?

Whatever your talent, whatever your resource, offer it to God, think outside the box, imagine previously unimaginable possibilities and be creative! Sure, there will be times when you feel completely inadequate to carry out the mission God has given you. At times, you'll be staring at odds of six to one or six hundred to one and you'll think, "What's the use! Why even try? I'm toast!"

But God has promised us that his grace is sufficient for us. In fact, he says that his strength is perfected in our weakness. The more hopeless the situation, the more dramatic his deliverance will be! (See 2 Cor. 12:9.)

In John 6, we find an instructive story: Jesus was walking beside the Sea of Galilee when a vast crowd came toward him. Seeing the people, Jesus turned to one of his disciples and said, "Where shall we buy bread for these people to eat?"

The disciple said, "Eight months' wages wouldn't buy enough bread for each person to have one bite!"

Then another disciple brought a boy to Jesus and said, "Here's a boy with five small barley loaves and two dried, salted fish—but how far will so little food go among so many?"

How did that disciple know about the boy and his little pittance of food? Probably because the boy went to the disciple, tugged at his sleeve and said, "Here, mister. Give this to Jesus. It isn't much, but he can have it if he wants."

So Jesus took the bread and the fish and told his disciples, "Have the people sit down." So the people sat down—about five thousand of them. And Jesus took the loaves and the fish, gave a prayer of thanks to God, then had his disciples distribute the food to the people. They all ate as much as they wanted—and there were twelve baskets of leftovers besides.

What's the point of this story? Is it simply that Jesus was the Son of God and a miracle worker? I believe there's much more to this story than that. I think that the practical importance of this story for our lives today is that if we will simply use what we have and offer it up to God with faith and a prayer of thanksgiving, he will return it to us multiplied many times over.

Clearly, that little boy with his little sack lunch never dreamed that he would be used to feed a multitude. But he gave what he had, and God took care of the rest.

And then there was David. Long before he was the king of Israel and "a man after God's own heart," David was a teenage boy armed with nothing but a sling and five smooth stones that he had taken from a riverbed. You probably remember the story from Samuel 17.

Though these events took place some four hundred years after Shamgar, the enemies were the same. It was the army of Israel versus the army of the Philistines, and they faced each other across a broad battlefield. The champion of the Philistines was a warrior named Goliath—a giant of a man, nine feet tall, with biceps as big and powerful as a V-8 engine. He wore two hundred pounds of armor and held a spear as long as a flagpole. At the sight of Goliath, the heart of every soldier in the army of Israel turned to quivering lime Jell-O.

In all of Israel, only one man wasn't afraid of Goliath—and he wasn't a man at all. He wasn't even a soldier. He was a teenage boy named David, a kid who tended sheep on his father's ranch. Yet David dared to walk right out onto the battlefield and insult Goliath to his face! At first Goliath laughed—but when he heard what David had to say, he became enraged.

"Today," the boy said, "the Lord is going to hand you over to me. I'm going to deck you and whack off your head. When I'm through with you, the whole world will know that there is a God in Israel, and that this battle is not a battle of swords or spears! This battle is the Lord's!"

Face red with fury, Goliath charged at David. Trusting fully in God, David charged at Goliath. As he ran, the boy reached into his pouch and pulled out a stone. He fitted that stone into the sling, whirled it around his head and flung it at the Philistine. The stone struck deep into Goliath's forehead. The Philistine fell like—well, like a stone. Then David bent down over Goliath, removed the Philistine's head and took it home with him as a trophy, just as he said he would.

The point of the story: God wants us to use what we have, even if it's just an ox-goad or five smooth stones. God has given us all the resources we need to gain the victory over the Philistines in our lives. His resources are our resources, available to us through prayer.

We are certainly no match for Goliath or for an army of six hundred Philistines. But God is more than a match for a million Goliaths or a billion Philistines! One person plus God is a majority, no matter how many Philistines are on the battlefield. How is that possible? Simple: because it's not a battle of swords or spears. This battle is the Lord's.

You and I face all kinds of Goliaths. We face giant-size challenges, obstacles, opponents, losses, failures and temptations. Every day, all around us, there are Goliath-size enemies that are bigger, meaner and far more powerful than we are. But there's not one of them who is a match for God. If we will just start where we are and use what we have, God will do the hard part.

In the story of David and Goliath, we catch a glimpse of God's marvelous creativity. Here we have Goliath, a mighty warrior of the Philistines, tall and powerful, covered with two hundred pounds of armor—but Goliath was not a creative thinker. He did all of his thinking inside the box.

But God had an outside-the-box plan to defeat Goliath, and he revealed that plan to the mind of young David. Conventional, inside-the-box thinking says, "Attack Goliath with the same old methods you've always used: cover yourself with armor, then grab your sword and hack away!" But unconventional, outside-the-box thinking says, "Why not attack Goliath in the way he will least expect it? Send a boy armed only with a sling and stones!"

God knew that David, with his well-practiced sling, could put a stone in the one unprotected place on Goliath's well-armored body: his forehead. A dozen men swinging a dozen swords couldn't have made a dent in Goliath's armor, but David, using a stone as if it were a laser-guided cruise missile, could hit Goliath in a vital spot with ease. So God sent a boy to do a man's job—and the boy got it done. That's creative thinking!

We've looked at two Old Testament stories that show how God always uses a creative approach to even the odds and win the battle. In the story of Shamgar, we see that God used an unlikely hero—a farmer armed only with an ox-goad—to defeat a vastly superior enemy. And in the story of David and Goliath, we see God using the same approach in a different way: instead of a farmer with an ox-goad, he uses a boy with a sling and some stones.

Do you see a pattern emerging? In the New Testament, Paul explained God's creative method this way: "But God chose the foolish things of the world to shame the wise; God chose the weak things of the world to shame the strong" (1 Cor. 1:27).

You may think, "Well, that was then, but this is now. God doesn't work that way anymore." Well, if that's what you're thinking, you're wrong! God still uses weak, foolish, unlikely people like us to accomplish his purposes! In fact, it's only when you admit your weakness, foolishness and lack of ability that God can truly begin to use you. As Paul wrote in 2 Corinthians 12:10, "That is why, for Christ's sake, I delight in weaknesses. . . . For when I am weak, then I am strong."

Be Prepared!

The story of David and Goliath also teaches us about the need to be prepared. God had been preparing David for this moment, just as he is preparing you and me for the trials and testing that we must undergo in life. When David volunteered to face Goliath in battle, he told King Saul, "I have been taking care of my father's sheep. When a lion or a bear came and took a sheep from the flock, I went after the beast, fought it and rescued the sheep from its mouth. If the animal turned on me, I seized it by its hair, whacked it and killed it. I have killed lions and bears, and this godless Philistine will die like one of them, because he has defied the armies of the living God."

When we hear the story of David and Goliath, we sometimes forget what went before the story. We assume that this boy David came out of nowhere and killed a giant, as if this was some pointless fairy tale. But David didn't come out of nowhere. God had been patiently preparing David for this crucial moment in Israel's history.

For years, David had tended his father's sheep and protected them from predators such as lions and bears. In the process, David had developed skills and confidence that would serve him well in defending the nation of Israel from the Philistines. David's skill with a sling didn't just happen. It was the result of hours and hours of practice. There's not a lot for a boy to do while standing in a field, tending sheep. So David spent much of his time practicing his aim with that sling. By the time he faced Goliath on that battlefield, he was an expert at hitting a target with accuracy and devastating force. God had prepared him well.

God will never call us to do anything that he does not enable, prepare and equip us to do. We may feel that we are in over our heads, but God knows that we can handle the challenge. Even if we fail, even if we think we have disappointed God and everyone around us, he knows what he's doing. When we fail, he has a lesson to teach us through our failure. Let God worry about the results. Your job is simply to start where you are, use what you have and do what you can.

Notice, too, that David also took a moment before going into battle to make sure he was well prepared for war. The Bible tells us that he paused at a stream, selected five smooth stones and put them in a pouch. As it turned out, he only needed one stone—but just to make sure, he chose five. He wanted to be ready in case his first four shots missed their mark. Though confident in the Lord, David was not over-confident. He left nothing to chance. Preparation is often the crucial difference between victory and defeat.

The importance of preparation is one reason I founded Student Leadership University (SLU), which is now in its tenth year. Student Leadership University is a four-year program that teaches middle and high school students the rules and tools of leadership, integrity, faith, time management and people skills. They're taught that they are young eagles; we tell them, "You don't ever have to settle when God intends you to soar." Our goal is to give young people a twenty-five-year head start in becoming leaders. Studies show that most leaders learn the essentials of leadership (such as people skills and time management) in their late thirties or early forties. We teach these skills to teens, so that they are prepared to lead by the time they are in their twenties. (For more information on SLU, see our Web site at *www.studentleadership.net.*)

When I think of preparation, I'm particularly reminded of one young man who is an alumnus of our SLU ministry program. His name is Luke Lin. I first met Luke almost a decade ago when he was a middle school student and SLU was in its infancy. Luke went through our program, which provides middle school and high school students with intensive leadership training from a unique Christian perspective.

Luke's youth pastor had told me that he was an accomplished pianist, and I soon heard the evidence with my own ears. In the daytime, Luke would sit in class, diligently taking notes. In the evenings, I would find him in the lobby of the Orlando hotel where we conducted some of our sessions. He would be sitting at the grand piano, playing classical music.

All around the lobby, people would stop, listen and wonder how someone so young could be so accomplished on the piano. I'm sure that most of the people who heard him thought he was hired by the hotel to play for the patrons' enjoyment! In reality, he had made arrangements with the hotel management to do his practicing in the lobby. His music was so beautiful, his technical artistry so confident, that it sounded like a concert—but to Luke, these were simply practice sessions.

Night after night, after our SLU sessions were dismissed and most of the students went back to their rooms to relax and watch TV, Luke went straight to the lobby to practice the piano for two hours straight. The next year, Luke went with his youth group to SLU 201 in Washington, D.C.—and again he maintained his nightly regimen of piano practice in the hotel lobby. The year after that, we held SLU 301 in Israel, and once more Luke's practice sessions dazzled the people who stopped by to listen.

Over the years, I watched Luke grow as a student leader, as a Christian, and as a skilled musician. The diligence of Luke Lin teaches us that it takes faithful practice and preparation behind the scenes, when no one is watching, in order to reach our goals. Luke could easily have taken a break from practice while he was at SLU. Instead, he chose to continue working toward his goal of becoming a concert pianist.

If we want to achieve great things tomorrow, we must fully dedicate ourselves to them today. Great achievements don't take place suddenly and instantly, even though it may seem that way to the casual observer. Great achievements are born in the private time spent in practice and preparation, as we daily keep faith with our dreams, our goals, and our mission in life.

I had a fascinating experience during the time I was working on this chapter. I was driving through the country club section of our city, heading for the driving range. There I happened to see none other than Tiger Woods, one of the greatest golfers who ever lived. Golf season was over, but he was at the driving range, hitting hundreds of balls, diligently practicing his drive. During the off-season, most players take time off to relax. But Tiger Woods was relentless in the pursuit of his game. In season or out of season, Tiger was working to improve his game.

I was amazed at my good fortune in getting to watch the legendary Tiger Woods as he honed his skills. But the very next day I was even more amazed. I had a meeting to attend at Arnold Palmer's beautiful Bay Hill Club and Resort. During the meeting, I looked out the window—and there was Tiger Woods again! As before, he was on the driving range, hitting ball after ball, practicing his swing, persistently preparing himself for the coming year.

Watching Tiger practice, I was reminded of this principle: If you want to look good in the spotlight, you have to work hard when no one is looking. You have to prepare—steadily, patiently, diligently—for the opportunities God will bring your way tomorrow.

Creativity is Our Birthright

If you are from my generation, the name Jethro Tull is probably familiar to you. It was the name of a famous blues-rock band from England in the late 1960s. But most '60s-era rock fans were unaware of the fact that the band got its name from a pioneering farmer-inventor of a previous era.

The *original* Jethro Tull was born in Basilson, Berkshire, England, in 1674. He was an ordinary man, a farmer like Shamgar, who had a profound impact on your life and mine. What did he do? Well, he created one of the most important agricultural revolutions in human history.

Like Shamgar, Jethro Tull was raised on a farm and spent many years of his life becoming proficient in every aspect of the agricultural industry. He was an educated man who had studied law. When circumstances prevented him from finishing his law degree, he returned to the farm.

In those days, crops were planted in much the same way they had been planted for centuries—by hand, one seed at a time. The farmer would drill a hole, drop in the seed, then smooth the soil over the seed with his fingers. As Jethro Tull was planting his fields in this time-tested manner, it occurred to him that there had to be an easier way to plant a few acres of corn! So he began to think outside the box—and an idea soon occurred to him.

He went to his toolshed and scrounged among the spare parts and tools he kept there. What did he find? An old unused pipe organ that he had dismantled sometime earlier, just to see how it worked. From pieces of that pipe organ, he devised a machine that could dispense seed three rows at once. It used a rotating cylinder to drop seeds at a steady, regulated pace. He came up with a drill that made holes in the earth and a device to cover the hole after the seeds were dropped in.

Jethro Tull's seed drill quickly became a widely used labor-saving tool that dramatically increased crop yields in Europe and America. Tull also developed the horse-drawn how (or hoe) to clear away weeds and prepare fields for planting. Jethro Tull started where he was, used what he had and did what he could. As a result, he revolutionized the way farmers grow our food and make their living.

The *Apollo 13* astronauts built a life-support system out of plastic bags, cardboard and tape. Jethro Tull took some parts from a dismantled pipe organ and built a machine that revolutionized agriculture. David used a sling and a stone to topple a giant. Shamgar turned an ox-goad into a lethal weapon. The lesson is clear: You can do a lot with a little—if you are willing to be creative.

We were made in the image of a creative God; creativity is our birthright. Don't ever say that you need to have the latest technology, the finest tools, the most expensive equipment in order to serve God and achieve your goals! You are creative! You can achieve great results with whatever resources you have.

When I think of creativity, I'm reminded of a young lady who went through one of our first Student Leadership University programs about a decade ago. Her name is Nikki Finch. While a junior in high school, Nikki made a decision to let God use her to make a difference in the world—and she wasn't going to be stopped by the fact that she was "just a teenager." While most of her friends were focused on listening to music or hanging out with friends, Nikki was learning how to be a leader. Here's her experience as she shared it with me:

> The story begins in July 1996 when I was seventeen. That's when I attended Student Leadership University 101 in Orlando. There I first grasped what could happen in my life if I would simply believe what Philippians 4:13 tells me: "I can do everything through [Christ] who gives me strength."
>
> In one session, Dr. Strack looked each student in the eye and asked, "If you had no limits on your life, what would you do? What goals would you set for your life?" He gave us ten minutes to write down our thoughts. Some students wrote that they would lose some weight, read more or try harder in school. Good goals—but I told myself, Nikki, think big! Dr. Strack said, "No limits!" What would that be like—living life without limits?
>
> I wrote down that I would like to meet the president of the United States and talk to him about Jesus Christ. Then I wrote that I would like to work undercover for the CIA. Then I wrote that I would like to be a national speaker for Students Against Drunk Driving (I was a leader in my high school's SADD chapter at the time).
>
> When I read my goals to the class, some thought they were unreachable. But I walked away from SLU 101 with the realization that nothing is unreachable when I have Jesus Christ at my side. I decided that I had

all the resources of the God of the Universe at my disposal, and I wasn't going to limit what He could do through me.

Even though I had set high goals and I believed I could reach them, my thinking was still limited in one way: I thought that I would not reach these goals for many years. I soon learned that God does not have an age requirement. He's ready to use us as soon as we start taking him seriously. Within a year of SLU 101, I reached many of the goals I set.

Though I still haven't gotten an assignment from the CIA yet, most of the so-called "unreachable" goals I wrote down at SLU 101 proved to be within my reach. I was selected to be the National SADD Student of the Year, and I traveled around the country speaking out on alcohol abuse. I met with the president to push for a national blood alcohol standard of .08.

Next, with the encouragement of family, friends and mentors, I took on a new alcohol abuse issue. I teamed up with New York's attorney general, Dennis Vacco, to end the practice of selling alcohol to minors over the Internet. I helped set up sting operations and lobbied Congress for federal legislation. We stood toe to toe with the alcohol industry—and we won.

In the past eight years, I have traveled to twenty-six states and three countries, speaking out on health and safety issues that affect my peers. I've held over forty press conferences, from the Capitol building to the White House, and I've appeared on news programs from NBC's Today show to CNN. I've met with President Clinton, lobbied Congress and sat on the boards of directors of three national nonprofit organizations. I earned a bachelor's degree from Florida State and spent a year serving in the D.C. inner-city schools with AmeriCorps. Young people can make a difference in the world if they will just open their minds to what God has planned for them.

The fact is, *anyone* can make a difference in the world. I can, you can, young people can, old people can, anyone can. All it takes is an open and creative mind, a touch of faith and the willingness to start where you are, use what you have and do what you can. If Nikki Finch can start on her high school campus, using only the limited resources that any high school student has, think of what you can accomplish if you will only open your mind and imagine the possibilities.

God is ready and waiting to use you to achieve great things. Now the only question is: Are you ready for God?

The Third Secret:
Do What
You Can

The Tale of Shamgar: Part Three

hamgar took the iron knife from his belt, then knelt down and held the weapon out to his son, Elishua. The blade gleamed like silver. Early that morning, Shamgar had honed the edge, then rubbed the blade with olive oil to keep the rust away. "Here, son," he said. "Look after your mother. If the Philistines come, trust God and use this knife. Do what you must. Do what you can."

"Yes, Father," the boy said. He was only eleven winters old, but there was a ferocity in his eyes that made Shamgar proud. "I'll take care of Mother."

Shamgar nodded. He wanted to say how much he loved the boy, but the lump in his throat would not let him speak. So he mussed the boy's hair, then stood and looked his wife, Dara, in the eye.

She was afraid. Not for herself. For him.

They were standing at the door of his house, in the shade of an old olive tree. His ox-goad leaned against the trunk of the tree. He took it in his right hand. "Well," he said.

"Well," she said. She didn't know what else to say.

"God will be with us," Shamgar said. He hefted the ox-goad.

Dara smiled sadly. "A wooden stick against iron swords."

"This 'stick' has tasted Philistine blood," Shamgar said. "It will do so again."

"Oh, Shamgar," Dara said, tears rolling down her cheeks. "Why must it be you? Of all the men in Israel, why you?"

"Because God put me here," Shamgar said. "He has given me a task, and no one else can do it. So I will do what I can."

"And die?"

"If God wills that I die today, then it is a good day to die." He winked and added, "But I will try not to."

Dara started to laugh, but it turned to tears. Shamgar pulled her close, kissed her, then said, "Take care of the boy. I'll come back to you. If I can."

Then he turned and walked down the path that led away from his farm and toward the Pass of Ma'arab. In his pack he carried hard bread and dried, salted deer meat. He knew where to find water and wild figs and grapes. He could live for weeks in the wilderness.

After two days of walking, he arrived at the pass. There was a high promontory overlooking the pass. Trees and brush grew on either side of the road. From the promontory, he could watch without being seen. From the trees and brush, he could attack without being suspected.

Shamgar knew that the Philistines had no history of massing large, well-disciplined armies as the Moabites, Egyptians and Babylonians did. Their approach to warfare was brutish and unsophisticated. They sent raiding parties of twelve to thirty men, and they were as noisy as Shamgar was stealthy.

He waited two days before the first Philistine patrol came lumbering through the pass. There were about twenty-five of them. He crouched in a shrub-lined pit a few yards from the road and listened to their heavy, clanking tread as they marched by. Then he jumped up and way-laid the last man in line, skewering him through the throat and drag-ging him off the road. The Philistine wasn't missed.

Shamgar bushwhacked the next man in line, clubbed and felled the next, and on and on until he had thinned the ranks of the Philistine patrol by half. He was about to attack once more when the last remain-ing man in line turned to say something to the man behind him—only to discover that he was now the last in line. He shouted, the entire line stopped—and the Philistines began beating the bushes, searching for this ghost who had somehow made half their comrades disappear. By the time the Philistines had found where he had hidden some of their dead, he was on the high promontory, watching from a safe distance.

More patrols came though the pass, only to meet the same fate or worse. One time, he had depleted a Philistine war party from thirty men down to three when they suddenly turned and saw the Hebrew avenger standing before them, ox-goad in hand. Shamgar was afraid— but he refused to show it. He charged at the commander, who barely had time to raise his sword before finding himself impaled on an ox-goad. Suddenly leaderless, the other two men fled. Shamgar had to chase them down in order to kill them.

Word quickly spread throughout the Philistine ranks that war parties that went into the Pass of Ma'arab never came out. Rumors spread that an invisible army of ghosts or demons haunted the oak groves in the pass—an army that fought on the side of the Hebrews.

Soon, the Philistines began avoiding the pass. They took a long and winding path to the west, toward the sea. For a while, that was a safer way for the Philistines to go and a number of patrols got through. But soon the Philistine raiding parties began disappearing along that path as well.

Shamgar used the chisel end of his ox-goad to make gashes in the trunk of an ancient oak that grew along the side of the promontory. With those gashes, he kept track of the number of Philistines he had slain. In a busy week, he sometimes added as many as eighty to a hundred gashes to the tree.

Eventually, the Philistines stopped coming up the path from the south. Shamgar waited one week, then another week. Finally, he was satisfied that the Philistine invasion was over. He could go home.

Along the winding path to his farm, Shamgar passed mounds of dead Philistines that he had piled up week by week. By this time, most of the armor-clad bones were bleached white, having been picked clean by vultures, carrion beetles and flies.

Shamgar had spent nearly three months in the wild, living off the land, killing and eating only animals that were clean according to God's Law—mostly doves, but also an occasional deer, antelope or wild goat. No matter how hungry he was, he refused to eat any unclean animals, such as rats, badgers, coneys or wild pigs. Shamgar wouldn't break the Law of Moses even to save his own life.

As he drew closer to his farm, Shamgar passed people he knew. Hardly any of them recognized him until he greeted them by name. Then they would look at him in astonishment and say, "Shamgar! It's you!" He wasn't sure if he had changed that much or if people were simply amazed that he had survived. In truth, it was both.

His face was gaunt, his cheeks were hollow, and his skin was nut-brown. The muscles of his arms and legs were more sharply defined, as were his protruding ribs. He had been a lean man when he left home three months before; now he was a sun-browned ghost of his former self.

When he finally topped the last rise before reaching his farm, he stopped and stared numbly. Spread out before him was a scene of devastation. His fields were burned to the ground. The ox pens were broken, and both of his oxen were gone. The stone-walled farmhouse was blackened and gutted by fire. Even the roof timbers were burned away. The Philistines had been to his farm and torched everything. Nothing was left, not even—

Where was Dara? Where was his son?

Shamgar swayed on unsteady legs, his mind a whirl of panic. An image of blackened bones in a burned-out house flickered through his mind, but he pushed it away. He prayed, *O Lord! Please don't let me find—*

But Shamgar couldn't bring himself to finish the thought. On legs that were like pillars of lead, he staggered down the road, toward the ruins of his house.

7

What Can One Person Do?

by Pat Williams

"The world's in a terrible mess, but what can one person do?"

You've heard words like those before. Fact is, one person *can change the world*—or at least a little piece of it.

One person can share a word of encouragement or a smile with another person who desperately needs it. One person can give an hour or a day or a lifetime to a worthy cause. One person can adopt a child or mentor a troubled teen. One person can speak up and defend another person who is being treated unjustly. One person can show love and forgiveness instead of hatred and bitterness.

Think of it this way: Somewhere there is a vitally important task that no one is doing. If you don't do it, then it simply won't get done.

You are not expendable. You are not replaceable. You are absolutely essential to God's plan. If you do not carry out the life mission God has given you, your work will simply go undone.

God has given you a mission in life, and only you can carry it out. What can one person do? You can start where you are. You can use what you have. And you can do what you can. Do that—and you'll be amazed at what he will do through you.

One April 21, 1855, a Sunday school teacher named Edward Kimball walked into Holton's Shoe Store in Boston. He saw a young shoe clerk wrapping shoes, and without even a word of introduction, he said to the clerk, "Young man, I want to tell you how much Jesus Christ loves you." The clerk listened, and Mr. Kimball talked. After a while, the young clerk got down on his knees and prayed, asking Jesus Christ to become the Lord of his life. That young clerk's name was Dwight L. Moody.

Moody became an evangelist and preached across the United States. In 1879, he went to England and held a series of evangelistic meetings there. One of those who came to hear Moody was a pastor named Fredrick B. Meyer. Prior to hearing Moody speak, Meyer believed that his purpose in life was to (as he put it) "increase my influence, make money, draw audiences and do philanthropic work." He didn't believe in the reality of a living, dynamic God who was truly involved in human lives.

All of that changed when Meyer heard Dwight L. Moody speak. The English pastor went to his knees and surrendered his life to Jesus Christ, and his ministry in the church was forever transformed. F. B. Meyer became a great preacher and author who influenced thousands of people to make a life-changing decision for Jesus Christ.

Meyer came to the United States and preached to packed auditoriums throughout New England and down the Atlantic coast. One of those who heard Meyer preach was J. Wilbur Chapman. Chapman's soul was so stirred by the Gospel that he decided to become an evangelist like F. B. Meyer.

J. Wilbur Chapman became involved with a number of Christian ministries, including an organization that merged the Christian Gospel with athletics, the Young Men's Christian Association (YMCA).

Through the YMCA, Chapman became acquainted with a former pro baseball player named Billy Sunday.

Billy Sunday had played for National League clubs in Chicago, Pittsburgh and Philadelphia in the late 1800s, and was the first player to run the bases in fourteen seconds. In 1886, he asked Jesus to be the Lord of his life through an outreach of the Pacific Garden Mission in Chicago. Five years later, he quit baseball (turning down salary offers that would have paid him more money per week than most people made in a year). Billy Sunday joined J. Wilbur Chapman's evangelistic organization, becoming a preacher and evangelist.

One place where Billy Sunday's preaching had a special impact was Charlotte, North Carolina. A group of Charlotte businessmen were so deeply impacted by Billy Sunday's ministry that they organized a committee to bring evangelists to Charlotte on a regular basis. One of the evangelists they invited was Mordecai Ham of Louisville, Kentucky.

In 1934, during one of Mordecai Ham's evangelistic meetings, there was a troubled young man sitting in the audience who was struggling with God. At the end of the service, that young man walked forward and prayed to ask Jesus Christ to take control of his life. That young man's name was Billy Graham.

No one knows for sure how many people Billy Graham has preached to in tents, auditoriums and stadiums over the years, but it is estimated at over a billion. Add in the numbers of people who have heard him preach via TV or radio, and the number becomes impossible to calculate.

What can one person do?

I doubt that Edward Kimball had any idea the chain of events he was setting in motion that day he told a young shoe clerk about the love of Jesus Christ. No one ever knows the long-range impact their words or actions may have. All we know is that we must start where we are, use what we have and do what we can—then leave the rest to God. Someday in eternity we may look back and be amazed at what those few words of ours ultimately accomplished.

Shamgar did what he could and he saved a nation. If you don't think you're up to saving a nation, then start a little smaller. Save a child. Save a tree. Save a whale. You can't do everything, but you can do something. So do what you can.

Let me suggest seven things you can do that can make a difference in your life and the lives of people around you. Do these seven things and you just might change the world.

1. Pray

Most of us think of prayer as a last resort, an act of desperation: "If all else fails, pray." But if we realized the true power and effectiveness of prayer, we would probably spend half our days on our knees. As Charles H. Spurgeon once said, "Prayer is the slender nerve that moves the muscle of Omnipotence."

Minister and devotional writer E. M. Bounds described prayer this way: "God shapes the world by prayer. Prayers are deathless. The lips that uttered them may be closed in death, the heart that felt them may have ceased to beat, but their prayers live before God, and God's heart is set on them. Prayers outlive the lives of those who uttered them; outlive a generation; outlive an age; outlive a world."

Bill Bright, the late founder of Campus Crusade for Christ and a man I was honored to know as a friend, once described prayer this way: "It is impossible to overexaggerate the importance of prayer: 'Whatever you ask in my name,' Jesus said, 'I will do it.' And whatever we ask, according to God's will, he will hear and answer. These are promises."

English preacher and author J. Sidlow Baxter put prayer in perspective when he wrote, "Men may spurn our appeals, reject our message, oppose our arguments or despise our persons, but they are helpless against our prayers." And Oswald Chambers, author of *My Utmost for His Highest,* said, "Prayer does not equip us for greater works. Prayer *is* the greater work."

How, then, should we pray? Are there specific components or steps to effective prayer? I believe there are. Based on my own experience with prayer, I would suggest these steps to an effective prayer life:

First, *start your day with prayer.* Oswald Chambers once said, "If in the first waking moment of the day you learn to fling the door back and let God in, every public thing will be stamped with the presence of God." As you greet the day, greet God. Ask him to walk with you throughout the day.

Second, *pray unceasingly.* Paul, in 1 Thessalonians 5:17, says, "Pray continually." You might think it's impossible to pray continually and unceasingly, but it's not. Every conversation between friends has its pauses, its quiet moments. So does prayer. Your conversation with God may have pauses that last a half hour, an hour, or more, but the conversation goes on. When you rise in the morning, as you stare glassy-eyed into your first cup of coffee, as you drive to work, as you pause to say thanks for your lunch, as you face a crisis at the office, as you drive home, as you greet your loved ones at the door, as you have dinner, as you relax before bedtime, as your head sinks into the pillow—

Talk to God. Listen to God. Remain in a warm, friendly, daylong, lifelong, unceasing conversation with your heavenly Friend, the Maker of the Universe, the Maker of you. He's available and he's listening, 24-7.

You'll probably find that the more you pray, the more you want to pray. You won't want to be out of his presence, his sight, his earshot, even for a moment.

Third, *pray from the heart*. Honestly tell God what you are thinking and feeling. Don't worry about using all the right religious words. You don't need to pray in old-fashioned King James English, as some preachers like to do ("Glorified art Thou, O Lord! My heart cryeth unto Thee!"). Just talk to God as you would talk to a close friend, to a loving Father. He doesn't care about your memorized phrases or religious clichés—he just wants to hear what's on your mind. Plus, he wants you to hear what's on his mind.

Praying from the heart also means: Don't hold anything back. Are you angry with God? Tell him. Yell at him, even. He can take it. In fact, he'd rather receive your honest feelings from the top of your lungs than to hear nothing but a chilly silence. If something good happens, and you feel grateful and joyful, tell him that, too. He'd love to hear about it. Nothing you say is going to shock God or make him turn his back on you. He loves you more than you love yourself.

Fourth, *pray specifically*. Tell God *exactly* how you feel, and *exactly* what you need, and *exactly* what you hope for. Sure, he already knows what we need. He knows our hopes and dreams. Tell him anyway. He likes to hear it from us.

When praying specifically, expect an answer. Remember, his answer might be "No," or "Not yet." Why? Because just as children sometimes ask for things that their parents know are not the best for them, we sometimes ask for one thing when God has something better in mind.

Even though God sometimes says "No" to our prayers, you'd be surprised at how often he says "Yes!" Like any loving parent, God would much rather say "Yes" to his children than "No." So pray specifically and watch for his answers. Better yet, keep a prayer journal and write down the requests you make—followed by the date that your request was answered. I guarantee that if you keep a journal of your prayers and God's answers, you'll be amazed and your faith will soar.

Fifth, *pray boldly and confidently*. The New Testament book of Hebrews tells us, "Let us then approach the throne of grace with confidence, so that we may receive mercy and find grace to help us in our time of need" (Heb. 4:16). Understand, I'm not saying that we should order God around or make demands of him. We need to pray with humility. But we should also go to God with confidence, knowing that he is merciful and gracious, and he wants to answer our prayers.

Jesus said, "So I say to you: Ask and it will be given to you; seek and you will find; knock and the door will be opened to you. For everyone who asks receives; he who seeks finds; and to him who knocks, the door will be opened" (Luke 11:9–10). In short, Jesus is saying that we should pray boldly and confidently, expecting God to act on our prayers. That is an ironclad promise from Jesus himself.

Sixth, *pray audibly*. You may have noticed that when you pray silently, "thinking" your prayers to God, your mind tends to wander, you get distracted—and you may even fall asleep! I guarantee that you won't fall asleep if you pray out loud.

You may feel a little odd at first when you pray aloud—you might feel as if you are talking to yourself. But there's something about talking audibly to God that enables you to focus, to pray with enthusiasm and intensity. Find a place where you can go to be alone, a place of solitude where you won't be overheard. Make that your refuge, your sanctuary, where you can go and talk—really talk!—with God.

Seventh, *pray obediently*. Someone once said, "When you pray, don't give God instructions. Just report for duty." We should come to God with an obedient mind-set, ready not only to present our requests to him, but also to receive our orders from him. If God is truly Lord of our lives, then we must come to him humbly and obediently, willing to go where he sends us and do what he asks us to do.

Many people are afraid to approach God this way. They fear God's will. They are afraid that God will ask them to do what they are afraid to do. And sometimes it's true that God will, out of his great love for us, ask us to move beyond our comfort zone in order to serve him and others. So we must pray for courage to face our fears and to obediently do God's will.

Pastor and author Max Lucado once wrote, "How did Jesus endure the terror of the crucifixion? He went, first, to the Father with his fears. He modeled the words of Psalm 56:3: 'When I am afraid, I put my trust in you' (NLT). Do the same with yours. Don't avoid life's Gardens of Gethsemane. Enter them. Just don't enter them alone."

Eighth, *pray collectively.* Join your prayers with the prayers of others. Jesus said, "Again, I tell you that if two of you on earth agree about anything you ask for, it will be done for you by my Father in heaven. For where two or three come together in my name, there am I with them" (Matt. 18:19–20). Certainly, God hears us when we pray to him one on one. But something special happens when two or more believers join their hearts and agree together in prayer.

Linebacker Peter Boulware of the Baltimore Ravens once said, "Prayer is like breathing to me. It is the key to life; it's talking to the Lord. It's not only me praying, but I have a lot of people praying for me, and I pray for other people."

Ninth, *pray forgivingly.* When Jesus taught his disciples to pray, he told them to say, "Forgive us our sins, for we also forgive everyone who sins against us" (Luke 11:4). Forgiveness is a critical component of effective prayer. A spirit of bitterness or anger blocks prayer; forgiveness keeps the channel of God's grace open and flowing.

NHL star Markus Naslund of the Vancouver Canucks recalls, "I was helping out at a Christian hockey camp. One of the kids asked me about my coach, and I said 'I'm not too fond of him.' Later, a lady came up to me and said 'Why don't you try this: Don't say anything negative about your coach. Just pray for him every day.' I thought, 'Yeah, I might as well. It's tough to dislike someone when you're praying for them.' So I started praying for my coach every day, and I felt a big stone lift off my heart. It was neat to see how the relationship has built up. My coach started playing me more and respecting me. In the end, we were like good friends."

Tenth, *leave the results to God.* Tony Dungy, head coach of the Indianapolis Colts, said, "With anything that comes across my desk, if I pray about it and ask for the Lord's direction, he's going to work those situations for his glory. It will be for the best, and it will succeed— maybe not the success the world would see, but success in his eyes."

It's true. What looks like success to God often looks like failure to the world. When Jesus prayed in the Garden of Gethsemane and asked to be spared the horrors of the cross, God the Father answered "No." So Jesus obediently submitted himself to the will of the Father.

The Roman soldiers nailed him to a wooden cross and suspended him between the earth and sky. There, he died. To everyone who watched him die, Jesus looked like an absolute failure. But God knew that the death of Jesus would produce success beyond anyone's ability to imagine.

So it is with us and our prayers. We must pray. We must ask for God's direction. We must trust him to work in all the situations of our lives. And we must leave the results to him. Those results will always be successful results in God's eyes—but they may not look like success to us, or to the people around us. None of that matters. Our job is to keep praying and trusting.

You may pray, "God, please keep my business from going bankrupt," or, "God, please save my marriage," or, "God, please don't let this be cancer." However God chooses to answer that prayer, it will be a success in his eyes, even if it looks like failure from a human perspective.

Don't assume that God didn't answer your prayer. Don't assume that he's gone back on his promises. Just leave the results to him and wait to see how the next stage of his plan for your life unfolds. Keep praying, keep listening, keep trusting.

2. *Think*

Before you take any action, first pray, then think. A surgeon was once asked, "If you only had five minutes to perform a lifesaving operation, what would you do?" His answer: "I would spend the first three minutes thinking and planning the procedure."

In a crisis, people often neglect to stop and think. "It's an emergency!" they say. "I have to act! I don't have time to think!" They don't realize that acting without thinking is likely to make the problem worse, not better. Thinking time is never wasted time. In fact, time spent thinking through all the possible solutions to a problem will probably save time, money and trouble in the end. Thinking could save your job, your reputation or even your life. Here are some suggestions for thinking about your problems in a more focused, effective, and productive way:

First, *think deliberately.* When faced with a problem or a crisis, don't just let your mind whirl around in a dither. Slow down. Take a deep breath. Get focused and centered. Think carefully, logically and deliberately about the situation. Analyze the issues. Clarify your goals. Plan your strategy. Ask yourself a series of questions to help reveal the sources and solutions of your problem, such as:

a. "What is the problem?" You can't begin solving the problem until you have clearly defined and understood the nature of the problem.

b. "What is the source or cause of the problem?" At this point, you're not trying to fix blame; you're trying to fix the problem. So don't ask, "Whose fault is it?" Ask, "Where did this problem originate? What are the possible causes?"

c. "What are the possible solutions?" Most problems don't have just one solution, but a range of potential solutions. Be creative. Explore a range of alternatives before settling on one single solution to the problem.

d. "What are the downsides of the various solutions?" Are there undesirable side effects to some possible solutions? This will help to eliminate unworkable solutions and narrow your range of options.

e. "What resources do I need to solve the problem?" Some solutions may turn out, on examination, to be too expensive to implement. Others might be easily and cheaply implemented with the resources you have on hand. This question, too, will help you to narrow your range of options down to the one or two best solutions.

f. "What is my decision?" Having followed the first five steps of this process, you will probably find that the final step—your decision—is a fairly easy one. Careful step-by-step thinking always makes the decision-making process easier and more effective.

Second, *think flexibly*. Never allow your mind to be set in concrete. Most problems have multiple solutions, and the best solution is often the least expected. As events change, as new information comes our way, we must always be ready to change our plans and revise our thinking. We must be nimble and responsive to every new and unexpected contingency that pops up in front of us. If a door slams shut in our faces, we need to open a window, scramble through and keep moving toward our goals.

Inventor Edwin Land once said, "New ideas are easy. Getting rid of the old ones is hard." In order to clear your mind of rusty, outmoded ideas, you must develop a habit of thinking flexibly.

There's no doubt in my mind that Shamgar must have had a flexible, agile mind. In the process of knocking off an army of six hundred Philistine invaders, he probably discovered fifty-seven ways of using an ox-goad that he had never thought of before.

Third, *think logically and with precision*. Sloppy thinking produces costly mistakes. So make a habit of checking everything twice. Be conscientious about thinking clearly, being sure of your facts, and using sound, logical reasoning in arriving at your conclusions.

Fourth, *think systematically*. Use a thinking system that works. Here are some suggestions for a systematic approach to thinking:

a. Set aside a daily, regular time (ideally, at least half an hour) for intense, focused thinking. Combine your thinking time with prayer time. Use this time for brainstorming new ideas or analyzing a problem.

b. Focus your thinking around your life mission, the grand goals you feel called to accomplish in your life, and the steps you must take to achieve those goals. Don't waste time thinking about trivialities. Don't daydream. Focus on what is truly important in your life.

c. Use pencil and paper, a journal or diary, or a computer to make your thoughts tangible and to provide a written record of your thought processes.

d. Set aside a specific place that is your thinking place—a room or a park or a rooftop where you can go and focus your thoughts without interruption. Leave your pager or cell phone behind and enter your sanctuary of thought.

Systematic thinking is powerful, effective thinking. Once you learn to think systematically and regularly, you will begin to see enormous acceleration in your progress toward your goals.

Fifth, *think big!* Think grand, bold, audacious thoughts. Brainstorm ideas and solutions that are so wild and startling that people will think you're crazy. When you successfully implement your big, bold ideas, people will think you're a genius! Great accomplishments are always preceded by great thoughts and great ideas. Don't be timid. Think big!

3. Set Goals

If you want to succeed like Shamgar, you must set goals, then move toward those goals in a deliberate and determined way. Goals give direction to your life. Goals enable you to chart your progress on the journey to your destination—the fulfillment of your life's mission. Goals give direction and purpose to life. If you have no goals, you are just marking time until you die.

John Maxwell once said, "Ninety-five percent of achieving anything is knowing what you want and paying the price to get it." Having clear goals is the best way to determine if you are making good use of your time. Whenever you engage in a certain activity, you can ask yourself,

"Does this activity move me toward my goals—or does it keep me from my goals?" The answer to the question makes it very clear if you should be engaging in that activity, or if your time could be spent more productively elsewhere.

Once you begin looking at your daily activities through the filter of your goals, you will see some remarkable changes in the way you live your life. You'll live each day in a much more focused, productive and satisfying way. When you know what you want to accomplish in life, you will no longer tolerate those time-bleeding, energy-draining activities that nibble away at your life and keep you from your goals.

You'll turn off the TV, watch fewer movies, waste less time reading the newspaper and become more selective in your social activities. As a result, you'll devote more of your life to the things that matter—and you'll see a marked acceleration toward your objectives in life.

You should have, first of all, a sense of mission, purpose and calling in your life—what I would call a *life goal*. Your life goal is the target at which you aim the arrow of your life. It is the destination you choose to reach in the journey of your life. When setting life goals, think big! Don't place any limits on your goals and dreams.

What if your goal is so big that it intimidates you? What if your dream is so vast that you don't even know where to begin? No problem! You simply break down your big life goal into a series of more bite-size goals that keep you moving forward.

If Shamgar had known from the outset that it was going to be one Hebrew farmer versus six hundred Philistines, he probably would have thrown up his hands and said, "Why even start? It's hopeless! It's humanly impossible!" The reason Shamgar was able to do what he did was that he broke his big goal ("I will save my nation") down into a series of smaller goals ("I will defeat these twelve or twenty

Philistines"). And he even broke those smaller goals down into even smaller goals ("I will skewer this big bruiser, then the next one, and the one after that").

You and I should approach goal-setting the same way. You can accomplish any "extreme dream" if you break it down into doable chunks. A marathon seems like a daunting challenge until you look at it as a series of twenty-six one-mile goals. Writing a book seems intimidating—until you realize that it's just a matter of persistently writing one chapter after another. Losing fifty pounds seems like an impossible task until we realize that it's just a matter of losing a pound a week for a year with a sensible diet and exercise plan.

My friend Rich DeVos, owner of the Orlando Magic and founder of the Amway Corporation (now an Alticor company), started by bottling his products in his own basement and selling them himself. By the time he retired, he had built his company into a seven billion dollar global operation. He was once asked how he and his partner, Jay Van Andel, did it. "All Jay and I ever did," he said, "was get up every day and go to work, and add another distributor, another product, another country."

So the way to achieve big goals is to break them down into little goals. Every step you make along the way enables you to mark your progress toward your "extreme dream."

Long-term goals look five to ten years into the future. They are clear, measurable goals with a long but definite deadline: "I will complete my novel within five years from this date," or, "I will move to Nepal and open a youth hostel by the end of this decade." Goals should never be fuzzy or vague; goal-setting should never be confused with "wishin' and hopin'." When you set a long-range goal, you should know exactly what you want to accomplish, when you expect to accomplish it and how you plan to get it done.

You should break your long-term goals down into *mid-range goals* that look a year or two into the future. Mid-range goals are intermediate steps that help advance you toward your long-range goals. Mid-range goals should be divided into *short-range goals* consisting of the various tasks you have to carry out over the next few weeks to move you along to your mid-range goals. And, of course, your short-range goals should be broken down into daily "Things to Do" lists.

What should your goals be? No one can decide that but you. It's not easy to set goals, but it's essential if you want to successfully complete your mission in life. A person with a clear set of goals can achieve practically anything in life. A person without goals is going nowhere.

Your long-range and life goals should be BIG. Don't be timid when you are setting goals for your life. Sam Walton, the founder of Wal-Mart, said, "I believe in always having goals and setting them high." And media magnate Ted Turner observed, "My father always said 'Never set goals you can reach in your lifetime, because there's nothing left after you accomplish them.'"

Goals should be written down, not just remembered. Written goals are visible, tangible and memorable. When you write down your goals, you can post them on your refrigerator or set them as the wallpaper on your PC. You want to keep them in front of you as a constant reminder. Writing down your goals is a good way of programming them into your conscious and subconscious mind.

When you set goals, set a deadline. A goal without a deadline is just a fantasy. Deadlines force you to focus on your goals in a persistent and concrete way. When you know you have to meet a deadline to achieve your goals, you tend to get up earlier, work harder and stay later to get your tasks done. Deadlines force you to prioritize and organize more effectively.

Florence Chadwick was a world-class swimmer who set a record in 1950 by swimming the English Channel (from France to England) in thirteen hours and twenty minutes—a distance of twenty-one miles at the Dover Straits. In 1951, she swam the Channel from England to France, becoming the first woman in history to achieve this feat from both shores.

In 1952, Florence Chadwick set out to conquer an even longer distance, the twenty-six miles between Catalina Island and the California shore at Palos Verdes. The water was icy and shark-infested, but she wasn't worried about the fins that circled around her. There was only one thing that worried Florence Chadwick: a blanket of gray fog.

She set out from Catalina and made good time during the first twelve hours of the swim. But then the fog closed in. After fifteen hours, unable to see the coastline, Chadwick conceded defeat and climbed into the escort boat. She later admitted that she simply lost her desire to press on. "It was the fog," she said. "If I could have seen land, I could have finished. But when you can't see your goal, you lose all sense of progress and you begin to give up."

How far was Florence Chadwick when she gave up on her quest? A mere one-half mile. She had covered *98 percent of the distance* to her objective, and gave up with *only 2 percent* of the distance remaining!

A few months later, she repeated the attempt—and she reached her goal in thirteen hours and forty-seven minutes, breaking a record set in 1927 by a male swimmer. Why was she able to reach her goal on the second attempt? Because the sun was shining and it was easy for Chadwick to keep her objective in view.

The same is true for you and me. We need to set specific goals, write them down and keep them always before us. Setting goals is a crucial part of starting where you are, using what you have and doing what you can.

4. Work Hard

It may seem like stating the obvious, but nothing of importance is ever accomplished without hard work. The hardest part of hard work is getting started. For writers, the hardest task of all is sitting down at the keyboard and typing that first sentence. For musicians, the hardest part about practicing is opening the instrument case. As J. R. R. Tolkien, author of *The Lord of the Rings* trilogy, once said, "It's a job that's never started that takes the longest to finish." The essential factor that separates successes from failures is the willingness and discipline to work hard.

Olympia J. Snowe, United States senator from Maine, acquired her strong work ethic from her aunt. She recalls, "My aunt used to say to me, 'Olympia, don't ever wait for me to ask you. Look around and see if there's something that needs to be done and do it.' So, guess what? Now, I can't sit still! As soon as I sit down, I find myself thinking, 'What needs to be done?' and I start doing it. I can't help myself."

I tell my children all the time that the two most important words in the English language are "What else?" As in, "What else can I do? What else can I offer? What else can I contribute?" If you are a "what else?" person, you will always be in demand, because there aren't very many of them out there.

Kemmons Wilson was nine months old when his father died. "I never knew him," Wilson recalled. "Early on, I was so hungry when I was growing up that I was scared that I might be hungry again. I became a hard worker. I enjoy working."

Born in 1913, Wilson was fourteen and making drugstore deliveries on his bicycle when he was hit by a car and nearly killed. His injuries kept him laid up for a year, and doctors said he would never walk again. Wilson proved the doctors wrong.

In 1951, Kemmons Wilson was vacationing with his family and he became incensed over the high price and poor quality of family motels. So he started his own chain of motels and called it Holiday Inn. He set high-quality standards, air-conditioned every room and offered a pool and restaurant at every location. In the process, he revolutionized the hospitality industry.

Wilson once wrote a pamphlet called *Twenty Tips for Success*. The first of those twenty tips: "Work only a half a day; it makes no difference which half—it can be either the first twelve hours or the last twelve hours." Wilson followed his own advice. Until shortly before his death at age ninety, Kemmons Wilson continued to put in twelve-hour workdays.

Legendary ad man David Ogilvy, founder of Ogilvy and Mather, said, "I admire people who work with gusto. If you don't enjoy what you are doing, I beg you to find another job. Remember the Scottish proverb: 'Be happy while you're living, for you're a long time dead.'"

Some people say that the ability to work hard can compensate for a lack of talent—to which the late, great British prime minister, Winston Churchill, replied, "The ability to work hard is, in itself, a talent." If you are able to work hard—and I mean ten, twelve, fourteen or more hours a day—then you will set yourself far apart from the great mass of humanity. You will distinguish yourself and you will earn great rewards. Why? Because, to put it bluntly, most people are lazy. Everyone wants to enjoy the lifestyle of the rich and famous, but few are willing to put in the hard work and sacrifice required to attain it. As Zig Ziglar once said, "There is no traffic jam on the extra mile."

Doak Walker was a four-time All-Pro halfback who led the Detroit Lions to two NFL titles (1952 and 1953). He once said, "No champion has ever achieved his goal without showing more dedication than the next person; working harder than the next person; making more sacrifices than the next person; training and conditioning himself more than the next person; studying harder than the next person; enjoying his final goal more than the next person."

Those who put out a 100 percent effort never have cause (or time!) for regrets. The person who puts out a 98 percent effort sometimes does. George Plimpton, in his book *The X Factor: A Quest for Excellence,* tells the story of Willie Davis, star defensive end for the Green Bay Packers in the 1960s. Today, Davis is a successful businessman, a radio industry CEO and a director on the boards of such companies as Dow Chemical, MGM and Sara Lee. Despite all of his success, both in and out of football, he has one major regret that haunts him to this day.

Davis was playing in a game against the Philadelphia Eagles. Late in the game, he saw an Eagles ballcarrier streaking down the far sideline. Davis knew he had the speed to reach him—but why bother? There were other Packers defenders who were in position to catch him. Why, Davis wondered, should he wear himself out when his teammates would surely bring the ballcarrier down? So Davis dogged it and let the runner go.

The Eagles ballcarrier slipped the Packers' tacklers and scored a touchdown. In the end, that score cost the Packers the game.

As he went to the locker room, all Willie Davis could think of was the fact that he had a chance to prevent that touchdown, but he let the runner go—just because he didn't want to work too hard. He had made a conscious decision not to put out the extra effort that, as it turned out, would have won the game. He knew he would live with that regret for the rest of his life.

That day, Willie Davis made a life-changing decision. As he told George Plimpton, "Never again would I come out of any situation wondering if I could have done a job better. That principle is as important to me today as it was then. Every day, I tell myself not to let an opportunity slide by that I could have taken advantage of."

We like to pretend that we are working at 100 percent of capacity every day—and that on those rare occasions when we stay a half hour after work or do a little work over the weekend, we are giving 110 percent. That was the attitude of a young Bill Walton when he was playing basketball for Coach John Wooden at UCLA. When Wooden told Walton that he needed to put out more effort, Walton said, "Coach, I'm already putting out 110 percent!" To this, Coach Wooden replied, "No one can give 110 percent! Don't you know anything about mathematics?"

It's true. Most of us actually get by with an effort that is closer to 50 or 60 percent of our capacity. If we manage to work up a little sweat, we think we are giving 110 percent, but we're really only at 70 or 80 percent. If we ever truly gave a 100 percent effort to reaching an important goal, we would find out that we are capable of achieving far more than we ever dreamed possible.

If you can discipline yourself to work hard, you can achieve just about any goal you set your mind to. If you feel that hard work is just too much of an imposition on your cushy lifestyle, then you must accept the fact that you will never rise above the level of mediocrity. To be a successful person, you must start where you are, use what you have and work very hard at doing what you can.

5. Compete Intensely

You've gotta love Shamgar's competitive spirit! He took on six hundred heavily armed, heavily armored Philistines—and he beat them!

People who make a real difference in the world are invariably people who are competitive.

Understand, a competitive person isn't merely someone who wants to win. A competitor wants to be the best. That's why people who cheat to win are not true competitors. They're frauds. True competitors don't compete to pump up their own egos or reputations. They compete to raise the level of their own performance.

To be a true competitor, you must love and respect your opponent. Why? Because your opponent forces you to elevate your performance and be the best you can be. Sure, winning is important—but excellence is even more important. The late Wayne Calloway, who was chairman and CEO of PepsiCo from 1986 to 1996, said, "Nothing focuses the mind better than the constant sight of a competitor who wants to wipe you off the map."

Pat Summitt, women's basketball coach at the University of Tennessee and a six-time NCAA Championship winner, put it this way: "Your competitors make you better. Having worthy adversaries stimulates your work ethic and brings out qualities you may not have known you had. Don't resent them. You should love your competitors and thank them. Competitiveness is what separates achievers from the average. Only by learning to compete can you discover just how much you are capable of achieving. Trust me, you have more within you than you realize. Competition is one of the great tools for exploring yourself and surprising yourself."

Paula Newby-Fraser is an eight-time Ironman Triathlon World Champion and has been acclaimed by ABC's Wide World of Sports as "The Greatest All-Around Female Athlete in the World." She said, "When you compete against someone of equal or greater ability, it can lift your energy and mental concentration to new heights. A certain degree of positive stress can be very beneficial and can motivate you to work harder. The key is to see your rivalry as your guiding light, as a tool you can use to find the potential within yourself. Instead of wishing a competitor ill fortune, the healthy athlete wants a rival to succeed so they both can rise to a whole new level."

Authentic competition is honest competition. Entrepreneur William Simon, who once ran for governor of California, said, "The whole point of free enterprise, of capitalism, is vigorous, honest competition. Every corner cut, every bribe placed, every little cheating move by a businessman in pursuit of quick plunder instead of honest profit, is an outright attack on the real free enterprise system."

In recent years, the advocates of so-called political correctness have tried to rid our society of competition, claiming that there is something fundamentally unfair about any system that produces winners and losers. After all, losing makes people feel bad! (And after all these years in the pro sports business, don't I know it!)

But the truth is that, try as we might, we can't root competitiveness out of the human spirit—nor should we want to. Competition is good for the soul. It's good for business, for sports, for education, for every human endeavor. Competition raises standards and produces excellence. Competition is here to stay.

In his book *Who Needs God?*, Rabbi Harold Kushner (author of *When Bad Things Happen to Good People*) tells the story of a young premed sophomore at Stanford. As a reward for his excellent grades in school, his parents gave him an expense-paid vacation to the Far East.

While in Asia, the young man met a guru who said, "By seeking after success, young man, you are destroying your soul. You study and study in order to get a better grade than your friend. Your idea of a happy marriage is to marry the prettiest girl in school, the girl all your friends want. You are constantly competing with those around you. People were not meant to live that way. Give up your striving. Join us here in the ashram, where there is no striving, no competition—only meditation, sharing and joy."

The young man found the guru's message persuasive, so he joined the ashram. He phoned his parents and told them about his decision. His parents were heartbroken. They urged their son to come back home and pursue a career in medicine, but he was adamant. "Sorry. I don't want all that striving and competition. I just want to live in the ashram and experience true peace and bliss."

Six months passed. Finally, the young man's parents received a letter from their son in the Far East. "Dear Mom and Dad," it read. "I know you weren't pleased with the decision I made, but I want you to know how happy I've been here in the ashram. For the first time in my life, I've found peace. Here there is no striving, no competition, no one trying to beat out the next guy. We all share everything equally, and my soul is experiencing true harmony and joy at last." He signed the letter, then added a P.S.: "One more thing—I've only been here six months and I'm already the number two disciple in the ashram! If I keep working at my meditating, I think I can be number one by June!"

You see? You can't get away from competition! And you shouldn't want to. Competition is about being the best. When you start where you are, use what you have and do what you can, make sure you do everything competitively, to the best of your ability. The competitiveness of Shamgar enabled him to beat six-hundred-to-one odds. A competitive spirit will enable you to swing the odds in your favor, too.

6. Persevere

Perseverance is more important than brains, skill, talent or luck. One of my most memorable lessons in the importance of perseverance came during the summer following my eighth grade year. I tried out for a semipro baseball team, and though all the other players were much older, I made the team. Even so, I was worried about whether I could really perform at the same level as the other players.

On the way to my first game, I rode in the backseat while my mother drove. My grandmother sat up front next to Mom. As we drove, we talked about my prospects with the team. "Well," I said at one point, "if it doesn't work out, I can always quit."

With a suddenness that startled me, my grandmother whirled around, jabbed one finger in my chest and said, "You don't quit! Nobody in this family quits!"

I got the message. And I didn't quit.

I am a father to nineteen children—four by birth, fourteen by international adoption (Romania, South Korea, the Philippines and Brazil), and one by remarriage. Because of my large family, people ask me all the time, "Are there any common traits you notice among all of your kids?" And yes, there is one trait I've seen in all my kids at one time or another: Whenever things get tough, they say, "I know how to fix that—I'll quit!"

It doesn't matter whether it's the swimming team or advanced math or an after-school job stacking boxes at K-Mart—when the going gets tough, kids want to quit. They want everything easy; they want the road of life to be as smooth as glass. So one of my most important missions as a father is to turn young quitters into persistent winners by convincing them that quitting is a permanent solution to a temporary problem.

I love to read—especially biographies of great people. I've read a ton of them, and I've discovered a common thread in the lives of all influential men and women: No matter what culture or period of history they lived in, they all had extraordinary obstacles to overcome; they all suffered setbacks, heartaches and defeats; and they all refused to quit.

Read the life story of any great individual—Abraham Lincoln, Eleanor Roosevelt, Winston Churchill, Martin Luther King, Jr., Walt Disney, Frederick Douglass, Helen Keller, Galileo, Louis Pasteur, Ludwig van Beethoven, Jackie Robinson, Gandhi, Rosa Parks—and you will see a person who possessed an inner intensity that absolutely refused to quit. These individuals would climb over, scramble around, tunnel under or simply dynamite any obstacle in their way. If at any point they had said, "I quit," we would never have heard of them.

As I write these words, I have run thirty-one marathons. A marathon, of course, is a cross-country footrace that is 26.2 miles from start to finish. It is one of the most punishing things you can do to the human body. People ask me, "Why do you put yourself through that kind of torture?" My answer: Running marathons is the best way I know to practice perseverance.

After the first eight or ten miles of a marathon, my body and head are screaming, "Stop this foolishness! Give it up! End this pain! Quit, quit, quit!" But unless you have run a marathon, you can't imagine the euphoric feeling of crossing that finish line. When you've run a marathon, my friend, you know that you can persevere!

Many years ago, an ambitious young employee of the Ford Motor Company sought out the boss himself, Henry Ford, and asked, "Mr. Ford, how can I be successful in life?"

Without hesitating, Ford answered, "When you start something, finish it."

Henry Ford knew the power of perseverance. He went broke five times before he finally succeeded in the automobile business. Though his successes were great, his failures were embarrassing. The very first Ford motor car had a glaring design defect: Ford forgot to install a reverse gear! But he knew how to achieve his goals—never give up. Never quit.

After a concert, a woman once came up to violin virtuoso Fritz Kreisler and said, "Oh, Mr. Kreisler, I'd give my life to play as beautifully as you!"

"Madam," Kreisler answered, "I have." To be a virtuoso at the violin or at anything else, you must persevere. Never give up, never quit.

Tom Monahan bought a struggling hole-in-the-wall pizza shop in 1960. The shop continued to struggle under his ownership for eight years—then he lost the entire business in a fire. The insurance company paid him ten cents on the dollar. He took the money, invested in a new pizza shop, and after two years fell behind in his loan payments and lost the shop to the bank.

In 1971, with debts of over $1.5 million, with his creditors threatening lawsuits, Monahan asked himself, "How can I turn this around?" The answer that came to him: home delivery. People could pick up the phone, call his shop and he would have the pizza delivered to the customer's home within thirty minutes.

Though we take pizza delivery for granted today, no one ever offered home-delivered pizza before Tom Monahan invented the concept. Today, his company—Domino's Pizza—has over 7,400 corporate and franchise stores in more than fifty countries. Tom Monahan is living proof that the key to success is perseverance—never give up. Don't quit.

Today, Michael Blake is a successful novelist and screenwriter. But for most of his life, he felt like a failure. He had left home at age seventeen, wrote more than twenty screenplays plus a number of novels and received nothing but rejections for twenty-five years. Still, he refused to give up.

At age forty-two, he finally made his first sale—a novel called *Dances with Wolves*. He had spent months working on it while living out of his car and washing dishes in a Chinese restaurant in Arizona. When he completed the manuscript, he dedicated it to his friends Viggo Mortensen and Exene Cervenka, with whom he had been staying for several weeks.

Actor-producer Kevin Costner bought the rights to the novel and hired Blake to write the screenplay. Costner's film of *Dances with Wolves* won the Academy Award as best picture for 1990. After years of failure and rejection, Michael Blake was finally on his way.

"Successful people," said motivational author Napoleon Hill, "usually find that great success lies just beyond the point when they're convinced that their idea is not going to work." And legendary boxer James "Gentleman Jim" Corbett, who KO'd the great John L. Sullivan in a grueling twenty-one-round fight in New Orleans in 1892, put it this way:

> *Fight one more round when your feet are so tired that you have to shuffle back to the center of the ring—fight one more round.*
>
> *When your arms are so tired you can hardly lift your hands to come on guard—fight one more round.*
>
> *When your nose is bleeding and your eyes are black and you are so tired you wish your opponent would crack you on the jaw and put you to sleep—fight one more round.*
>
> *Remembering that the man who always fights one more round is never whipped.*

An ancient proverb from China puts it even more succinctly: "Fall down seven times; get up eight." There is one quality that is common to all successful people, all people who have ever made a difference in this world: persistence.

They started where they were, they used what they had, they did what they could. They never surrendered. They held on and held out. They refused to quit.

7. Serve Others

Penelope Duckworth, Episcopal chaplain to Stanford University in California, was once on a night flight aboard a 747 to California. She got up from her seat to go to the lounge to get a soft drink, and an older woman asked if she could join her. The woman had a European accent and a quiet manner. The two women sat in the lounge and talked. The woman told Duckworth that her son was a teacher in Boston and her daughter lived on a kibbutz in Israel. "Oh," said Duckworth, "then you're Jewish."

"No," the woman said, "I'm a Christian, but I raised my daughter as a Jew."

Duckworth was intrigued. "Why would you raise your daughter in a different faith than your own?"

"I am from Poland," the woman said. "During the early days of World War II, the Nazis came to our village and rounded up all the Jews. We didn't know about the extermination camps. We didn't know what the Nazis were going to do to the Jews. But we knew that whatever the Nazis did would be terrible.

"I was shopping near the train station when the Gestapo arrived to take the Jews away on the train. I saw some soldiers putting Jewish villagers into cattle cars. One Nazi soldier was pushing a Jewish woman toward the train, and her little girl was following just a few steps behind. The soldier saw the child and asked the woman, 'Is that your daughter?' The Jewish woman pointed straight at me and said, 'No, the child is hers.'"

Duckworth's jaw dropped. "You took the woman's daughter? You raised her as your own?"

"If I hadn't," the woman said, "she would have died in the camp, just as her mother did. I raised her as my own daughter—but I raised her to be Jewish, as her mother would have. What else could I do? What would you have done?"

We have all been placed on this earth for a reason. And our reason for living has nothing to do with being rich or famous or successful. It has nothing to do with what we gain. It has everything to do with what we give. It has to do with the things we say and do and sacrifice in order to serve others.

In 1922, Agnes Gonxha Bojaxhiu, a twelve-year-old girl in Skopje, Macedonia, felt that God was calling her to devote her life completely to him. She left home at the age of eighteen and joined the Sisters of Loreto, a community of nuns. After training in Dublin, she went to India in 1931, where she took her vows. She taught at St. Mary's, a convent school in Calcutta. After years of teaching, she felt God calling her to a ministry beyond those convent walls.

Agnes rarely got outside the convent and caught only occasional glimpses of the poverty and suffering that filled the streets of India. In 1948, she obtained permission to leave the convent school and devote herself to working in the slums of Calcutta. She started an open-air school for the children of the slums. During those early years of service to the children of Calcutta, Agnes Bojaxhiu acquired a new name— Mother Teresa.

In 1950, Mother Teresa founded a new order, the Missionaries of Charity, to serve the needs of people who had been forgotten by society. In those early days, the outreach of the Missionaries of Charity was primarily to people with leprosy, who were dying alone and friendless in the streets of Calcutta. Today, the Missionaries of Charity has a global ministry, helping the poorest of the poor, victims of natural catastrophes, homeless people, shut-ins, alcoholics and AIDS sufferers.

Often, when Mother Teresa traveled to speak in Europe and America, her listeners would be moved with a desire to do something, anything, to help the poor and suffering people of Calcutta. They would come to her after her talk, or they would write letters, saying, "I want to help the poor and the lepers. Please tell me how I can join you and work with you in Calcutta."

Mother Teresa would always respond with a simple four-word reply: "Find your own Calcutta."

Mother Teresa knew that people sometimes got caught up in the emotion of the moment when they heard the heart-tugging story of some poor leper or an orphaned child on the streets in India. She knew that some people had romanticized notions of going to an exotic city and finding meaning in their lives by ministering to needy people. She knew that emotionalism and romanticism were the wrong reasons for wanting to serve others. So she once said these words: "Stay where you are. Find your own Calcutta. Find the sick, the suffering and the lonely right there where you are—in your own homes and in your own families, in your workplaces and in your schools. You can find Calcutta all over the world, if you have the eyes to see. Everywhere, wherever you go, you find people who are unwanted, unloved, uncared for, rejected by society—completely forgotten, completely alone."

And she was right. Calcutta is all around us—if we have the eyes to see. It may not be as appealing to our sense of adventure to serve the needy people we find right in our own neighborhoods. We would much rather help the needy in Calcutta than the needy in central Los Angeles or the south side of Chicago, in Camden, New Jersey, or Hialeah, Florida, or Milwaukee, Wisconsin, or Oakland, California. But the need is all around us, and the need is great.

As someone has said, we are all guilty of the good that we do not do. We have received so many blessings from God that are beyond our ability to deserve or repay, and service to others, as Lord Halifax (Churchill's foreign secretary during World War II) once said, "is the rent we pay for our room on earth."

But what should we do? How should we serve other people? By now, you shouldn't even have to ask such a question. You simply start where you are, use what you have and do what you can. If you have money, give money. If you have time, give time. If you have love, give love.

When showing love to others, begin by serving the people you don't like. Jesus put it this way: "But love your enemies, do good to them, and lend to them without expecting to get anything back. Then your reward will be great, and you will be sons of the Most High, because he is kind to the ungrateful and wicked" (Luke 6:35).

And in *Mere Christianity,* C. S. Lewis said, "Do not waste time bothering whether you 'love' your neighbor; act as if you did. As soon as we do this we find one of the great secrets. When you are behaving as if you loved someone, you will presently come to love him. If you injure someone you dislike, you will find yourself disliking him more. If you do him a good turn, you will find yourself disliking him less."

A life of serving others does not mean that we must impoverish ourselves or that we cannot be successful in terms of our finances and our careers. John Wesley, the godly founder of the Methodist church, was deeply involved in ministering to the poor and the outcasts of his society. In a 1760 sermon called "The Use of Money," he said, "Gain all you can, save all you can, give all you can. Do all the good you can, in all the ways you can, to all the souls you can, in every place you can, at all times you can, with all the zeal you can, as long as you can."

John Wesley was saying to us in words the same thing Shamgar says to us through his actions: Start where you are, use what you have, do what you can. When John Alexander was president of InterVarsity Christian Fellowship, he used to ask students a penetrating question: "What have you done this past year to make a helpful difference within one mile of your home?"

Ouch! That is a painful question, isn't it?

The truth is that there are hurting, suffering, friendless, hopeless, needy souls within a mile of your doorstep, within walking distance, perhaps right next door to you. You don't have to go to Calcutta. Find your own Calcutta. Find someone to serve. Find someone to love. Find someone to save. St. Francis of Assisi once said, "Start by doing what is necessary. Then do what is possible. Suddenly, you are doing the impossible."

Shamgar did what he could, and he saved his nation.

What can you do, right where you are? And how soon can you do it?

No Other Plan

by Jay Strack

I recently had the privilege of spending time with the family of the slain civil rights leader, Dr. Martin Luther King, Jr. I enjoyed getting to know Ms. Coretta Scott King and Martin Luther King III, one of their four children. They showed me Dr. King's archives, including his school records from Morehouse College in Atlanta, Georgia, where he graduated in 1948 with a degree in sociology.

As we looked together at one of his semester grade reports, I was surprised to note that his lowest grade was in (of all things) public speaking! We all enjoyed a good laugh over that, given his legacy as one of the great public speakers of our time. Even more ironic was a comment in the margin, where his professor commented on the low grade he had given. "Martin," the professor wrote, "if you continue to use such lofty and flamboyant language, you will never be very effective in your public speaking."

I wonder if that professor was watching his former student on television, August 28, 1963, when he stood on the steps of the Lincoln Memorial, and his voice rolled across the vast crowd of people of many races. I wonder if that professor remembered that comment when he heard Dr. King say, in words that were lofty and flamboyant, yet movingly unforgettable:

> *I have a dream that my four children will one day live in a nation where they will not be judged by the color of their skin but by the content of their character. . . . I have a dream that one day every valley shall be exalted, every hill and mountain shall be made low, the rough places will be made plain, and the crooked places will be made straight, and the glory of the Lord shall be revealed, and all flesh shall see it together. . . . This will be the day when all of God's children will be able to sing with a new meaning, "My country 'tis of thee, sweet land of liberty, of thee I sing. Land where my fathers died, land of the pilgrim's pride, from every mountainside, let freedom ring." . . . When we let freedom ring, when we let it ring from every village and every hamlet, from every state and every city, we will be able to speed up that day when all of God's children, black men and white men, Jews and Gentiles, Protestants and Catholics, will be able to join hands and sing in the words of the old Negro spiritual, "Free at last! Free at last! Thank God Almighty, we are free at last!"*

I'm glad Dr. King did not listen to his professor at Morehouse College, but continued to preach in those lofty, flamboyant phrases that lifted our hearts and filled our eyes with a vision for a world beyond hatred, injustice and racial division. Because he rejected that advice, his great words are now burned into our hearts and into our history books.

I'm sure that Shamgar had to deal with the same kind of well-intentioned but misguided advice in his day. I can imagine Shamgar's neighbors, and perhaps even his family, saying, "Don't be a fool! You can't take on the entire Philistine army by yourself! You don't even have any armor or a decent spear or sword! You have nothing but an ox-goad! You're crazy to even try! You'll be killed!"

In view of the odds against him, this would be sound, logical advice. It only stands to reason that a warrior going up against six-hundred-to-one odds is bound to lose and be killed. If the Philistines captured him, he would probably be tortured to death. But Shamgar knew he had to do what he could, even if it cost him his life. He would win if he could—but win or lose, he would be faithful to God and to his nation.

There is an ancient proverb that states, "One who says that something cannot be done should not stand in the way of the one doing it." A much more recent proverb agrees: "Lead, follow, or get out of the way."

With the best of intentions, people will tell you, "Don't waste your time writing that book," or, "Don't waste your money starting a business right now," or, "Don't waste your compassion on those people," or, "Don't waste your life serving others when you could use your talent to become rich and influential." Most of the bad advice you'll receive in life comes with a side order of good intentions.

But what good are good intentions if they only serve to keep you from your goals? When people give you bad advice (however well-intentioned), simply thank them for their concern, then get on with the work God has given you to do.

People and Duct Tape

Some of the worst advice you'll ever receive actually comes from right inside of you. It comes in the form of self-doubt, self-criticism, and self-accusation. In Exodus 4, when God chose Moses to deliver the people of Israel from slavery in Egypt, Moses protested. "O Lord," he said, "I have never been eloquent. . . . I am slow of speech and tongue." Some scholars believe that the phrase "slow of speech and tongue" refers to a speech impediment—perhaps a problem with stuttering. Regardless of the reason why Moses hesitated, we know that Moses lacked confidence as a public speaker. He felt overwhelmed by the one thing he could not do well.

But God replied, "Who gave man his mouth? Who makes him deaf or mute? Who gives him sight or makes him blind? Is it not I, the Lord? Now go; I will help you speak and will teach you what to say." In other words, don't focus on what you can't do. Instead, focus on the One who has the power to enable you to do anything. Your job is to start where you are, use what you have and do what you can—and God will give you the power to do it.

Like Moses, we are easily overwhelmed by what we can't do instead of simply doing what we can. When God gives us a task or a mission to complete, we look at our resources and say, "No way! I'm not up to this! I could never do anything like this!"

But God sees the big picture, even when we can't. He says to us the same thing he said, in effect, to Moses: "You think you can't do this; but with my power working in you, I know you can do anything. You just do what you can, and I'll do the rest. Don't be so focused on what you can't do that you fail to do what you can! Just start where you are, use what you have, do what you can—and it will be enough. I will not ask you to do more than you can handle."

There are times when we all feel as insignificant as a single grain of sand on the beach. We think, "What can I do? I'm just one little person. I don't have much to offer God. I don't have much in the way of talent or resources."

Yet it is right here, in our feelings of powerlessness and insignificance, that the three secrets of Shamgar demonstrate their power in our lives. God doesn't call us to be talented or powerful or rich in resources. He simply calls us to start where we are, use what we have and do what we can. That's all he ever calls us to do, and he never calls us to do any more than that.

By simply doing what we can, as Shamgar did, we may be able to save a soul, or a life, or a neighborhood, or a cause, or a nation. You never know. And the best news of all is that we don't have to worry about the results, because the results are God's business. Our part is to simply do what we can.

You may think, "But it's too late for me. I've been sidelined too long. I'm too old to get in the game. Let me just sit here and be God's benchwarmer."

Perhaps that's what Shamgar thought when God first called him to take on the challenge of the Philistine invasion. We don't know how old Shamgar was when he heard God's call, but it's possible that he had been sitting on the bench for quite a long time, waiting for a chance to get in the game. After all those years pushing a plow, looking at the south end of a northbound ox, did Shamgar really have what it takes to launch a guerilla campaign against the Philistines?

Shamgar didn't know. There was no way he could know. He had never done anything like that before. There was only one thing Shamgar knew for sure: win, lose, or draw, he had to do what he could.

What about Shamgar's lack of training in the art of war? How could a farm boy do a soldier's job?

Well, consider this: A 1998 study conducted by scientists at the Lawrence Berkeley National Laboratory in California, reports that duct tape has thousands of practical uses, but the one thing it should not be used for is sealing heating ducts—the very task it was designed for!

Duct tape is a vinyl tape with embedded threads for strength and a rubbery waterproof glue for tackiness. People have reportedly used duct tape to tape wires and cables to the floor, repair cracked windows, fix broken book bindings, repair broken taillights, fix patio furniture and vinyl siding, patch seat covers, repair eyeglasses and even remove warts. But duct tape is not very good for sealing ducts.

The Berkeley Lab (a U.S. Department of Energy national laboratory) conducted tests on a number of heating and cooling duct sealants to find out which worked best under realistic conditions. According to Berkeley Lab researcher Max Sherman, "We tried as many different kinds of duct sealants as we could get our hands on. Of all the things we tested, only duct tape failed. It failed reliably and often quite catastrophically."

What's the point? Simply this: people and duct tape will surprise you. They often perform better at tasks they were not intended for than the tasks in which they should logically excel! A woman with a degree in art history could end up running a dot-com business. A man with an MBA could end up in the pulpit, preaching every Sunday. To the surprise of all who knew him, a farmer named Shamgar ended up as a military genius, a national hero and a judge over Israel. You never know. People and duct tape are full of surprises!

You may think you were born to be a farmer, a shoe clerk, a banker, a stockbroker, a computer programmer, a teacher or an actor—but God may have a better idea! You might discover that he has a plan and a purpose for your life that you never imagined. If you start where you are, use what you have and do what you can, you may find yourself accomplishing things you never dreamed you could do. It may not be what you planned to do with your life, it may not be what you trained for in college, but it will be what God created you to do, what you were meant to do.

And if God created you to do it, you are going to love it! The task or mission God has for your life will fit you like a glove.

Low-Intensity Conflict

Shamgar, you may recall, was the third judge in Israel. The first two judges, Othniel and Ehud, were military men who won great military battles. Othniel went to war and won a major battle over the army of the king of Aram. As a result of Othniel's victory, the land of Israel was at peace for forty years.

The second judge in Israel was Ehud, a brilliant strategist who personally carried out an assassination plot against the evil King Eglon of Moab. Then Ehud led the army of Israel into battle against the army of Moab, killing ten thousand enemy soldiers in a single day. Not one Moabite soldier escaped. The land of Israel experienced eighty years of peace after Ehud's victory.

Then we come upon this statement in Judges 3:31: "After Ehud came Shamgar son of Anath, who struck down six hundred Philistines with an ox-goad. He too saved Israel." The writer of Judges mentions Shamgar almost as a footnote or an "Oh, by the way" sort of remark.

Shamgar didn't conquer the nation of Aram or the nation of Moab. He didn't lead an attack that slaughtered ten thousand men in a single day. Shamgar engaged in what the Pentagon calls "low-intensity conflict" or guerilla warfare. The Pentagon has other names for guerilla warfare: "insurgency," "special warfare," "limited politico-military struggle" and so forth. That is not the kind of warfare that gets a whole chapter in the history books. Usually, as in Shamgar's case, low-intensity conflict only rates a footnote.

The U.S. Army Training Manual FC 100–20 (May 1986) says that low-intensity conflict "is generally confined to a specific geographical area and is often characterized by limitations of armaments, tactics and level of force." Well, an ox-goad certainly qualifies as a limited armament. One man alone taking on an army of six hundred certainly qualifies as a limitation of tactics and level of force. So Shamgar was a guerilla fighter. And guerilla fighters never get the glory that five-star generals get.

We don't know who wrote the book of Judges, though some Bible scholars think it was probably the prophet Samuel. In any case, it would seem at first glance that Shamgar might easily be justified in being a bit miffed at his biographer. After all, Shamgar saved Israel, just as Othniel and Ehud did—and he did it alone, armed only with an ox-goad! Isn't that worth at least one full chapter of narrative? But no! Two scattered verses are all Shamgar gets.

In fact, I think God may have been trying to drive home a point by confining Shamgar's story to those two little verses. Unlike Othniel and Ehud, Shamgar didn't win a big spectacular battle. We don't know how long it took Shamgar to rack up six hundred notches on his ox-goad, but it almost certainly didn't happen in a single day. In all likelihood, he won a long series of skirmishes, spread out over weeks or months, if not years.

We can compare the book of Judges to the history of World War II. Open any book on that war and you can find detailed accounts of the most famous battles—Anzio and Monte Cassino, the London Blitz, the Battle of the Bulge, D-Day, Leyte Gulf, Midway, Guadalcanal, Iwo Jima and on and on. But what about the lesser-known battles that also helped decide the war? The victories of the Filipino guerillas over the Japanese at Balete Pass and Ipo Dam? Or the almost forgotten battles of the Free French guerillas against the Nazis in the Sahara?

Shamgar's victory was one of those unnoticed, nearly forgotten battles of the Bible. And your battles and mine are much like his.

Every day, we fight our battles for God. Not big, headline-grabbing battles that leave us covered with medals and glory, but small, low-intensity conflicts that usually go unnoticed by the world. We fight our battles against temptation, against our own character flaws or laziness, against our own sins and bad habits. We fight our low-intensity conflicts against poverty and ignorance. We fight by mentoring or adopting a child. We fight by teaching a Sunday school class or helping a teacher in an overcrowded classroom. We fight by volunteering our time and our resources and our compassion.

We don't get noticed for fighting these little battles and winning these little victories. We don't get medals or glory. But these victories all count in the larger war. God sees, he remembers, and he will reward us for our faithfulness and our devotion to duty.

While we fight our battles for God and for others, it's important that we don't compare ourselves with others. We shouldn't say, "If I can't do what Mother Teresa did, if I can't fight in the big social or political or spiritual battles like Martin Luther King, Jr., or E. V. Hill, or Billy Graham, or Dietrich Bonhoeffer, then I can't do anything of value. I'm no good to God. I'm no good to anyone." We shouldn't compare ourselves to anyone else. Maybe you can't do what someone else does, but they can't do what you do either.

God has put you in a strategic position on the front lines of his war for human souls. Plant your feet, hold your ground and fight your battle. Start where you are, use what you have and do what you can— and it will be enough. Just stay at your post and fight the battle he has assigned to you, and he will take care of the war.

How to Listen Like Shamgar

Expectant parents spend weeks searching through baby name books, carefully considering every name from Aaron and Aaliyah to Zane and Zahara. They want to know not only how the name sounds, but what it means. No parent would want to give their child a beautiful-sounding name only to discover that the name is Gaelic for "dumber than dirt" or Swahili for "face like a pig."

Similarly, companies pay millions of dollars to PR firms, advertising agencies and market research professionals to come up with just the right names for their products and corporate identities. The right name can be worth billions. The wrong name can be a marketing disaster, as General Motors discovered when it tried to sell its Chevy Nova automobile in the Latin American market (*no va* in Spanish means "it won't go").

The names of people in the Bible are frequently used to describe that person's attributes, family history or a promise that is foretold about the child's future. Many times, a person's name becomes a self-fulfilling prophecy, a preview of the person's life and accomplishments.

For example, in Genesis 17, God makes a covenant with a man named Abram, saying, "You will be the father of many nations. No longer will you be called Abram [which means "Exalted Father"]; your name will be Abraham ["Father of Many"]." And in 1 Samuel 25, we meet a man named Nabal, described as "surly and mean in his dealings," a man so obnoxiously stupid that he actually insults David, his king. Verse 25 tells us that Nabal "is just like his name—his name is Fool, and folly goes with him." For many characters in the Bible, it's all in a name.

Shamgar's name is no exception. The name Shamgar gives us a fascinating glimpse into his character. Though Bible scholars are uncertain as to the exact derivation of Shamgar's name, it probably comes from the same Hebrew root word as the name of the Hebrew prophet Samuel. The name Samuel literally means "he hears God," and it comes from a root word that means "to listen with the intent of obeying an order." It refers to a way of listening that implies willing obedience, discernment and understanding. It is a way of listening to God that profoundly characterized the lives of Shamgar, Samuel and other heroes of the faith.

Shamgar's name tells us that he was a man who listened to God, then obediently went out and did what God told him to do. So the question that confronts us in the life of Shamgar is this: How well do *we* listen to God? How responsive are we to his voice? How obedient are we to God's will?

In our media-drenched age, we are surrounded by voices that shout for our attention, our time, our resources, our energy and even our souls. We need to learn how to shut out these distracting voices so that we can hear the voice of God speaking to us. We need to remember that prayer is a two-way street, and we need to listen as Shamgar did—with a willing and obedient spirit, eager to go wherever God sends us and to do whatever he commands.

When you pray, do you do all the talking? Do you address God as if he is your personal genie in a bottle, talking to him only about your needs, wants and problems? Or do you stop to listen for the voice of God? I'm not saying that his voice will come to you in audible words. Most likely, it will come to you quietly, in the form of an urging, a sense of assurance or direction, a reminder of a person you need to talk to or a task that needs to be done.

When we pray, we need to remember that God is God. Yes, he's our Friend, Counselor, Helper and Comforter, but he is also our Lord, Master and Maker. The Bible tells us how we should pray. For example, in Psalm 46:10 God tells us, "Be still, and know that I am God." And Jesus, in John 10:27, says, "My sheep listen to my voice; I know them, and they follow me."

Shamgar listened to God in the stillness of his own spirit. He heard the voice of God and he followed God's leading. As his name implies, Shamgar had a mind and will that was ready and willing to respond in obedience to the voice of God.

In order to listen to God, we need to stop listening to the bad advice and counsel of the world around us. The world is like a carnival, filled with sights and sounds and bright lights, with dozens of carny barkers shouting at us from their booths, "Try your luck! Don't miss out! Hurry, hurry, hurry, step right this way!" And we're tempted to try this, and look at that, and enter here and pay our money there—and soon we find that our pockets are turned inside out, our souls are wasted and we have been played for fools.

All around us, books and magazines, TV shows and movies, friends and peers are calling to us, trying to sell us false values, destructive philosophies, deceptive belief systems. We are surrounded by a cacophony of voices, trying to pull us away from a lifetime of service to God, trying to drown out the voice of God.

That is why, when we pray, we need to be still—and listen.

Ears Full of Cotton

In *He Still Moves Stones*, Max Lucado writes, "Ignore what people say. Block them out. Turn them off. Close your ears. And if you have to, walk away. Ignore the ones who say it is too late to start over. Disregard those who say you'll never amount to anything. Turn a deaf ear toward those who say you aren't smart enough, fast enough, tall enough, big enough—ignore them. Faith sometimes begins by stuffing your ears with cotton."

Abraham Lincoln stuffed his ears with cotton and listened to God, not the people around him. If he hadn't, America might be two countries today—one nation free and the other comprising slave-owners and slaves. Lincoln succeeded in ending slavery and holding the nation together—but he wasn't always the Great Emancipator. Earlier in his career, he was a great failure!

Before becoming president, he failed at two businesses and lost six elections. He failed at his first business in 1831, was defeated for the legislature in 1832, had his second business failure in 1833, suffered a nervous breakdown in 1836, was defeated for speaker in 1838, was defeated for elector in 1840, was defeated for Congress in 1843 and again in 1838, was defeated for the Senate in 1855, and was defeated for vice president in 1856—all before finally winning the presidency in 1860.

After his crushing loss in 1855, he said, "The path was worn and slippery. My foot slipped from under me, knocking the other out of the way. But I recovered and said to myself, 'It's a slip and not a fall.'" All of his well-intentioned friends begged him not to run for president—he would only humiliate himself. But Lincoln had learned to listen to the voice of God, not the voices of defeat and discouragement.

Walt Disney stuffed his ears with cotton. His father was a harsh and critical man who continually told young Walter to quit wasting time with his doodling and his drawings of farm animals. One of his teachers told him to stop making such ridiculous drawings in class—after all, she said, "Flowers don't have faces!"

At age seventeen, Walt served with the Red Cross ambulance corps in France, immediately following World War I. When he returned home, his father offered him a job in a Chicago jelly factory at twenty-five dollars a week—good money in 1918. Walt said, "I don't want to work in a jelly factory. I want to be an artist."

"Drawing silly pictures isn't a real job," his father replied.

But seventeen-year-old Walt Disney had a dream, and he wouldn't let his father pour cold water on his dream. He went to Kansas City and applied to be a cartoonist with the Kansas City *Star*; the editor turned him down for being too young. Unfazed, Walt went back the next day and applied for a job as copy boy; the advertising manager turned him down for being too old. So he applied at the Kansas City *Journal*, which also rejected him.

Walt finally got a job at a Kansas City commercial art studio earning $50 a month. There, he met a young cartoonist named Ub Iwerks, and the two teenage artists soon founded their own cartoon studio. While Walt and Ub were conducting their first crude experiments with animation, Walt made friends with a little mouse who sometimes ventured out of a hole in the wall. That mouse eventually found his way onto the animation cels that Walt and Ub drew, becoming world-famous as Mickey Mouse—

And the rest is animation history.

Of course, Walt still had to deal with people who said that his dreams were impractical. When he dreamed of creating the first full-length animated feature, all the Hollywood experts predicted failure. When he wanted to build the world's first theme park, the experts said he would be broke within a year. Even Walt's wife Lillian and brother Roy tried to talk him out of his boldest dreams. But Walt refused to listen to the critics, the naysayers, the doomsayers and even his own family.

Those who predicted failure were silenced when *Snow White and the Seven Dwarfs* was released and when Disneyland proved successful beyond even Walt's own expectations. Walt Disney is a household name today because he refused to listen to his critics and his well-intentioned friends.

History is filled with great people who were told they would never amount to a hill of beans. Thomas Edison, probably the greatest inventor of all time, was once called a "dunce" and labeled "addled" by one of his teachers. Albert Einstein flunked math in his youth and was labeled a slow learner by several teachers. Fortunately, both Edison and Einstein stuffed cotton in their ears and proceeded to change the world!

And then there was the Great Caruso. When he was a young man taking private voice lessons, Italian tenor Enrico Caruso was told that he would never succeed as a singer. "Your voice is like glass," said his teacher. "It cracks on the high notes. It is like gold at the bottom of the Tiber River—not worth digging for. I suggest you save yourself much pain and embarrassment and give up trying to be a singer."

But Caruso would not listen and would not give up. At his 1904 debut in Barcelona, his performance was greeted by hissing and booing. After a while, the loudest of his hecklers got up and left, and the remaining audience listened to him in chilly silence. At the end of the performance, there was no applause.

Later, when he sang at the opera house in Salerno, conductor Vincenzo Lombardi came to Caruso's aid. Whenever Caruso attempted the high B-flat in the "Flower Song" from *Carmen*, his voice broke like Maynard G. Krebs saying "Work!" Lombardi could see the relentless determination in Caruso, and he patiently helped the young singer build a "top" to his voice.

Caruso went on to perform at the Teatro Lirico in Milan, where enthusiastic crowds cheered the amazing range of his newly extended voice. Word of his triumph spread around the world, and offers soon poured in from England, America, Russia, across the continent and throughout Italy—including opera houses where he had previously been booed off the stage. Enrico Caruso ruled the opera world for decades to come, and after he died, one music critic observed, "The source of Caruso's existence lay only in himself. He was himself the great work of art—the masterpiece."

Theodor Geisel was born in Springfield, Massachusetts, in 1904. Though he liked to draw, he hardly seemed destined for greatness. His high school art teacher told him, "You'll never learn to draw." His Dartmouth College fraternity voted him "Least Likely to Succeed." He went to Oxford to pursue an advanced degree in literature, but dropped out due to boredom and restlessness.

He returned to the States and drew cartoons for a struggling magazine (the publication was so cash-strapped that it paid Geisel in shaving cream and soft drinks instead of money). He also drew comic advertisements for the insecticide Flit. In 1936, he wrote and illustrated a wildly imaginative book for children called *And to Think That I Saw It on Mulberry Street*. He submitted the book to one publisher after another; it was rejected *forty-three times*. Finally, the book was published for him by a friend, but it only sold a few thousand copies in its original printing.

In May 1954, *Life* magazine published a startling report on the problem of illiteracy among American schoolchildren. One reason cited by the report: children's books were boring and children didn't want to read them. Geisel decided to take up the challenge. He decided to write a book that would hold children's interest, but would only use a basic vocabulary of 220 words. It took him a year and a half to write it. He published that book under a pen name, which has since become world famous: Dr. Seuss. That book, *The Cat in the Hat,* sold 500,000 copies in 1957, its first year.

In 1960, publisher Bennett Cerf bet Theodor Geisel fifty dollars that he couldn't write a book using only a fifty-word vocabulary. Geisel won the bet by writing another hugely successful book, *Green Eggs and Ham* (though Cerf never paid off on the bet).

During his lifetime, more than 210 million copies of his Dr. Seuss books were sold. Fortunately for children everywhere, when Theodor Geisel's art teacher and college fraternity predicted failure, and when forty-three publishers rejected his work, he refused to be deterred. Dr. Seuss stuffed cotton in his ears, started where he was, used what he had and did what he could.

In your life there are people who should have been your cheerleaders and encouragers. Instead, they have told you that you can never succeed at anything, so why even try? Even if those people are no longer in your life, even if they have been dead for years, you can still hear their voices, berating you and making you feel terrible about yourself. It's time to stuff cotton in your ears and start listening to God.

The Creator of the Universe has made you with a purpose in mind. He has created you for a reason, and he has given you a mission to carry out. And there is nothing you lack. God has equipped you with everything you need to begin unwrapping the gift of the rest of your life. All you have to do is start where you are, use what you have and do what you can.

A Victorious Martyr

There is a moving story in Mark 14 that tells us a lot about the third success secret of Shamgar—do what you can. In that story, Jesus came to the village of Bethany, near Jerusalem, and stayed in the home of a man named Simon the Leper. While Jesus was at the dinner table, a woman entered the home carrying a jar carved from pure alabaster, a delicate translucent stone. The jar contained a very expensive perfume.

The woman approached Jesus and did something startling: she deliberately broke the jar of perfume. She could have simply removed the stopper from the jar, but she chose to break it. Then she poured the contents of the jar onto the head of Jesus. The fragrance of the perfume filled the entire house.

Some of the other people who were present became angry with the woman. They berated her and said, "Why did you waste that entire jar of perfume? It could have been sold for more than a year's wages! The money could have been given to the poor!"

"Leave her alone!" Jesus said. "Why are you bothering her? She has done a beautiful thing for me! You can help the poor anytime you want—but I'm not always going to be here with you." Jesus knew that, in just a few days, he would be taken out and nailed to a Roman cross.

Then Jesus said something fascinating. "This woman," he said, "did what she could."

She did what she could!

Somehow, she knew that Jesus was about to die. She knew that his body would be broken and his life would be poured out. So she symbolically broke that beautiful alabaster jar and poured out the contents on his head, so that it gave off a beautiful fragrance. She couldn't keep Jesus from being betrayed, handed over to the Romans and crucified. But she did what she could.

How long had she been saving that precious jar of perfume? How long had she kept it hidden, so that no thief would ever find it? Perhaps it had been given to her as a gift when she was born; she might have saved it all of those years to use on her wedding day. We don't know. But we do know that when she broke that jar, she sacrificed something that was incalculably precious.

She did what she could.

And when the people around her criticized her and attacked her and insulted her, Jesus silenced them and commended her. "She did what she could," he said. "She poured perfume on my body to prepare me for my burial. I tell you the truth, wherever the gospel is preached throughout the world, what she has done will also be told, in memory of her."

And Jesus was right, wasn't he? Just now, the story of this woman and her sacrifice has been told yet again in these very pages. She did what she could, at great personal cost. And Jesus said it was enough.

Four centuries after Jesus died, there lived a man named Telemachus, a monk in Asia Minor (modern-day Turkey). He felt God urging him to go to Rome, though he didn't know why. After weeks of walking, he arrived in Rome. He found a carnival atmosphere throughout the city, for it was the time of one of the Roman festivals. Telemachus asked what all the excitement was about, and the people told him that the gladiators would be fighting that day in the Coliseum. Everyone was going to watch the entertainment.

Telemachus wondered: was this why God had sent him to Rome? He followed the crowd to the Coliseum. History does not record how many people were there that day, but we do know that the Coliseum could hold as many as 80,000 spectators. Armored, sword-wielding gladiators came out into the arena. They were condemned prisoners, slaves and soldiers of other lands who had been taken captive in wars of Roman conquest. Their job was to fight and kill and die—all for the amusement of the crowds.

As the "entertainment" was about to begin, a horrified Telemachus witnessed what the poet Longfellow once described:

"O Caesar, we who are about to die
Salute you!" was the gladiators' cry
In the arena, standing face to face
With death and with the Roman populace.

Then, all around the arena, the battles began. Gladiators hacked and flailed at each other. Men fell screaming in death agony. Some cursed. Others begged for death.

In the stands, the crowd roared with bloodlust, laughing and cheering as men died. Telemachus jumped up and shouted, "In the name of Christ, stop!" But his voice was drowned by the roar of the crowd.

Telemachus made his way down the steps toward the arena floor. As he went, he shouted, "In the name of Christ, stop!" He found a way down out of the stands and into the blood-soaked arena. He tried to place himself between a pair of combatants, shouting, "In the name of Christ, stop!" They shoved him out of the way and continued fighting. But Telemachus continued to tug at them and plead with them.

The crowd became furious. Spectators called for the death of this meddling stranger. Finally, one of the gladiators turned his sword on Telemachus and ran him through. As Telemachus fell to the ground, he shouted one last time, "In the name of Christ, stop!" Then he died.

Some accounts say that the crowd was stunned to silence by the death of this good man. Other accounts suggest that the battles continued around the dead body of Telemachus. The truth has been blurred by the mists of time.

But we do know this: the Roman emperor, Honorius Caesar, heard about the death of Telemachus. He issued a proclamation calling Telemachus "a victorious martyr" and he forever banned the bloody spectacle of the gladiator battles. No gladiator contests were ever held in the Roman Coliseum after that day.

Telemachus was just an isolated monk from Asia Minor. He was no one special. He had no political power, no fame, no wealth. But he had his convictions and a calling from God to go to Rome. He didn't know what God wanted him to do there, but he knew that God wanted him there for a reason. In Rome, his body was broken like an alabaster jar. His life was poured out into the dust—a terrible waste, some would say.

But God did not think the life of Telemachus was wasted. As the Bible tells us, "Precious in the sight of the Lord is the death of his saints" (Ps. 116:15). The willing, obedient sacrifice of Telemachus resulted in his own death—and the saving of many lives. His sacrifice produced a sweet fragrance that filled the city of Rome—a fragrance of Christ, a fragrance of love.

Telemachus did what he could and it was enough.

My friend, think of what you could do if you were willing to listen to God, to start where you are, to go where he sends you, to use what you have, to do what you can. Telemachus transformed Roman society by following in the footsteps of Jesus. It cost him everything he had, including his life—but what a difference he made!

What are you willing to sacrifice to make a difference in your world?

Walking Without Legs

While my friend Bob Wieland was studying at the University of Wisconsin, LaCrosse, he was negotiating for a job as a pitcher with the Philadelphia Phillies. But Bob's pro baseball career was interrupted before it even started when he received a letter of greetings from Uncle

Sam. It was 1969, and the U.S. government had decided he was needed in Vietnam.

While in Vietnam, he became involved in a fierce firefight. When one of his buddies was wounded, Bob ran to his aid—but he didn't see the 82 mm mortar round that was right in his path. He stepped on it, the round exploded and Bob lost both of his legs. He was taken to a field hospital where the doctors pronounced him DOA—dead on arrival. But a few minutes later, someone noticed that Bob still had a pulse.

He had arrived in Vietnam weighing 200 pounds and standing six feet tall. He returned home weighing only 87 pounds, his body almost cut in half, a double amputee. Some people thought that Bob's life was over. Bob disagreed. He decided that, even without his legs, he could still do what he could.

The moment the doctors released him from intensive care, Bob started concentrating on his rehabilitation. To compensate for the loss of his legs, Bob began strength training on his arms and upper body. He wasn't going to be immobilized by a mortar round. He was going to go wherever he wanted, even if he had to get there by walking on his hands.

In 1977, weighing just 122 pounds, Wieland competed in the United States Power Lifting Championship. He broke the world record by lifting 303 pounds—then was told by the judges that he was disqualified. Someone checked the rule book and found that all contestants were required to wear shoes. Bob's quick reply: "Wouldn't you know? Today *would* be the day I forgot my shoes!"

Using a pair of special pads to cushion his fists, he has completed some of the most amazing treks in history. Beginning in September 1982, Bob actually walked all the way across America on his hands. He began his "Spirit of America" walk at Independence Hall in Knotts Berry Farm, and he completed his journey at the Vietnam Memorial in

Washington, D.C., in 1986. The entire walk, accomplished entirely on his hands, took three years, eight months, six days and nearly five million "hand steps."

He walked over concrete freeways, steel bridges, asphalt streets and gravel roads—and he did it all by simply putting one hand in front of the other. He continued his trek regardless of ice storms or desert heat. Sometimes his way was lined with cheering spectators, but there were also times when people heckled him. On one occasion, a carful of rowdy teens drove by, pelting him with water balloons.

When a reporter asked him what kept him motivated for such a long and arduous hike, he replied, "The Bible says, 'Delight yourself in the Lord and he will give you the desires of your heart.' That's what keeps me going."

In 1988, Bob became the only double-amputee to compete in the demanding Ironman Triathlon in Kona, Hawaii. He completed the grueling multisport competition by using his arms to propel him one step at a time toward the finish line. In 2004, he completed the Los Angeles Marathon with a time of 173 hours and 45 minutes. He has also "run" the New York Marathon and the Marine Corps Marathon. He has broken the world record for the bench press four times; in 1993, he stunned the world by pressing 507 pounds. He has twice completed a 6,200 mile bike circuit across America.

Bob was recognized as "The Most Courageous Man in America" by the NFL Players Association and the Jim Thorpe Foundation, has served as a consultant to the President's Council on Physical Fitness and Sports and much more. But even more amazing than Bob's feats of physical endurance is his incredible faith.

He credits his achievements to the Lord who gives him the strength to take each step. He lives joyfully and gratefully, because every new day is a gift of the abundant grace of God. Bob easily could have sunk into bitterness and despair, like the wheelchair-bound Lieutenant Dan in the movie *Forrest Gump*. But Bob Wieland wanted nothing to do with self-pity. He made a deliberate choice to start where he was (a VA hospital), use what he had (two good arms) and do what he could (months of intensive therapy and training, followed by one incredible feat after another). Bob didn't just want to settle—he wanted to soar!

What about you? What do you want to do with the rest of your life? And what's stopping you? What are the obstacles in your way? What are the barriers you have to cross in order to reach your goal? Bob Wieland is living proof that most of the obstacles and barriers we face are only in our minds. As he says, "I lost my legs, not my heart." If a man without legs can do what he's done, then you and I have no excuses.

Life is a marathon. You may not think you can cross the finish line, but I know you can. You can overcome any opposition, any obstacle, even six-hundred-to-one odds, to reach your goal. All you have to do is follow the example of Shamgar, Martin Luther King, Jr., Abraham Lincoln, Walt Disney, Enrico Caruso, Dr. Seuss, Telemachus and Bob Wieland. All you have to do is start where you are, use what you have and do what you can.

If you do that, it will be enough.

God has a plan for this entire universe, and you are a part of that plan. He knew you by name before he even created the world. When he fit together all the millions of pieces of his eternal plan, he saved a piece with your name on it. There's a task that God has called you to do. I don't know what that task is, but I do know this: only you can do it. No one else can take your place. If you don't do it, then it won't get done.

There is an ancient fable that tells of a time after Jesus was crucified and rose again. On the day of Pentecost, he was taken up into heaven.

Upon his arrival, the angels gathered around and asked him how his work would continue on the earth without him.

"Oh," Jesus said, "I have a plan. I have left my disciples on the earth. They will share the Gospel with other people. Those people will hear the story of my love for them, and they will become my disciples, too. And they will tell other people, who will tell other people, who will tell other people. So faith will spread around the world, and many will come to believe in me. That is my plan."

The angels blinked in surprise. "You mean," they said, "you are trusting human beings to carry out your plan? You know how unreliable they are! You know how easily they become discouraged and give up!"

"Yes," Jesus said, "I know all that."

"But what if they let you down? What will you do then?"

"I don't know," Jesus said. "I have no other plan."

It's true. Jesus has entrusted his entire plan for the human race to us. You and I each have our role to play. If we do not do what God has called us to do, then no one will do it.

So we must do what we can, because the plan is us.

And there is no other plan.

The Tale of Shamgar:
Part four

S hamgar leaned against the doorway, staring at the blackened interior of the single-room house that had once been his home. The sun glared down through the rectangular open space where the roof had once been. The charred stumps of the roof-beams jutted from the walls. Within the house, not a stick of furniture remained. All was cinders and ash.

Are they here? he wondered. Are the ashes of their bodies mingled with the ashes of this house? Or were they captured and led away by the Philistines?

He took a few steps inside the house, his sandaled feet wading through mounds of soot. Shifting his ox-goad to his left hand, he crouched down and scooped up a handful of cinders. He let the black powder fall between his fingers like sands in an hourglass.

"Dara?" he said hoarsely. "Elishua?" In his mind, he could hear their voices answer him—"Shamgar!" "Father!"—as if from a great distance.

He reached into the ashes once more, feeling around for anything solid—and his fingers closed around something long and narrow, like the bone of a child. He held his breath and lifted the thing out of the ashes. He looked at it for several moments before he recognized it: an iron rod, part of the lampstand that had stood in the corner of the room. He breathed again.

Feeling around in the debris, he found other things—an iron cooking pot, a fragment of a bowl, Dara's clay spindle that she used for making thread. Were these shards and ashes all that remained of his family? Again, he seemed to hear their voices—"Shamgar!" "Father!"

He straightened, and his heart beat faster. He turned and went to the doorway, looking out. His vision blurred.

Dara and Elishua!

They were running across the blackened earth, arms outstretched, calling his name. He dropped the ox-goad into the pile of ashes and ran to meet them. He put one sinewy arm around his wife and the other around his son, and he hugged them to himself, feeling their warmth, covering them with kisses, praising God that they were alive—alive!

"Shamgar!" Dara said, weeping and laughing. "I thought you were dead!"

"You thought I was dead?" Shamgar said, touching his wife's face with his grimy fingertips, leaving tracks of soot where he touched her, yet thinking her beautiful nonetheless. "I thought you were both dead! How did you—"

Elishua pulled something from the sash that bound his tunic, and he held it out to Shamgar. A gleaming iron knife. "Here is the knife you gave me, Father," the boy said. "I wanted to use it on the Philistines, but Mother said we had to hide instead."

Wonderingly, Shamgar took the knife. "When did the Philistines come?" he said.

"They came at night, more than a month ago," Dara explained. "God woke me when they were still far away. Elishua and I could hear the clanking of their armor. We escaped into the oak grove and hid among the trees while the Philistines burned everything."

The boy made a contemptuous face. "They burned our house and took our oxen away!" He spat upon the ground.

Dara repressed a giggle. Elishua had so much of his father in him.

"In the morning," Dara said, "after the Philistines had gone, we went to the house of Giddel the Potter. We have been staying with him, waiting for you to return. This morning, Izhar the Levite came to the house and said you had been seen on the road from the south. He said you were coming home! So we ran as fast as we could! I'm just sorry we weren't here to meet you, and that the—" She paused, then burst out laughing.

"What?" said Shamgar.

"I'm sorry I left the house in such a mess," Dara said. "I guess I'm not a very good housekeeper!"

A few days later, Shamgar's neighbors gathered and celebrated his victory over the Philistines. They helped Shamgar rebuild his home, and they purchased two young, strong oxen to replace the pair he had lost.

Shamgar continued to farm his land. But now he was more than just a man of the soil. He was acknowledged by all to be God's chosen leader and judge over the land of Israel. In humility and wisdom, he served God and his people to the end of his days.

He had done what he could. He had saved Israel.

And it was enough.

Epilogue

by Jay Strack

I don't know if the following story actually happened or if it is a parable. But it makes a powerful statement about your life and mine.

It is said that an artist once painted a picture called "The Chess Player." The painting depicted two chess players, the devil and a young man. The devil is shown with an expression of triumph as he moves a chess piece and is about to call "checkmate." The young man's face is filled with horror and despair, for when he loses the game, he also forfeits his soul.

One day, the great nineteenth-century chess master, Paul Morphy, visited the art gallery where "The Chess Player" hung. As he studied the painting, he became very excited. Calling for a chessboard and pieces, Morphy arranged the board in the same configuration as shown in the painting. Then he said, "Look! The young man thinks he is checkmated—thus." And he moved the devil's black piece into position.

Then, after a dramatic pause, the grand master moved a white piece. "You see? With one move, I have set the young man free!"

So it is with you and me. In this game called Life, we face formidable opponents and great opposition. You may think you have lost, but God is the Grand Master of the Game of Life. He offers you a move that will set you free. No matter what opponents or obstacles you face right now, there is still one crucial move you can make.

You can start where you are, use what you have and do what you can. My friend, it's your move.

Resources

Feel free to contact Dr. Jay Strack at:

Dr. Jay Strack
Student Leadership University
7380 Sand Lake Rd., Suite 100
Orlando, FL 32819
PH: 407-248-0300 ext. 16
Fax: 407-248-0301 fax
E-mail: *jstrack007@studentleadership.net*

If you would like to schedule Dr. Strack for a speaking engagement, please e-mail him directly at the above address. You may also visit the Student Leadership University Web site at:

http://www.studentleadership.net/

You can contact Pat Williams at:

Pat Williams
c/o Orlando Magic
8701 Maitland Summit Blvd.
Orlando, FL 32810
PH: 407-916-2404
pwilliams@orlandomagic.com
Visit Pat Williams' Web site at:
http://www.patwilliamsmotivate.com/

If you would like to set up a speaking engagement for Pat Williams, please call or write his assistant, Diana Basch, at the above address or call her at 407-916-2454. Requests can also be faxed to 407-916-2986 or e-mailed to *dbasch@orlandomagic.com.*

We would love to hear from you. Please send your comments about this book to Pat Williams at the above address or in care of our publisher at the address below.

Thank you

Peter Vegso
Health Communications, Inc.
3201 SW 15th Street
Deerfield Beach, FL 33442
Fax: 954-360-0034

About the Authors

PAT WILLIAMS is senior vice president of the Orlando Magic of the NBA, a basketball team he co-founded in 1987. Pat has been involved in professional sports for forty-three years. He is one of America's top motivational and inspirational speakers and the author of thirty-five books. He and his wife, Ruth, live in Winter Park, Florida. They have nineteen children, including fourteen adopted from four foreign countries. Their children range in age from 19 through 32, and their first two grandchildren arrived in 2004.

JAY STRACK has authored nine highly acclaimed books. He's a dynamic speaker and founder of Student Leadership University. He speaks to more young people than anyone in America and has addressed more than 10,000 school assemblies. He is in demand as a speaker to corporate groups, government agencies, and professional basketball, football and baseball teams. He has spoken to audiences across the nation and in twenty-two countries around the world. Dr. Strack has been highly commended for his work in keeping young people off drugs. He served on the President's Anti-Drug Task Force under presidents Ronald Reagan and George H. W. Bush.

JIM DENNEY is a professional writer with more than sixty books to his credit, both fiction and nonfiction. He is the author of *Answers to Satisfy the Soul, Quit Your Day Job!* and the "Timebenders" science fantasy adventure series for young readers (*Battle Before Time, Doorway to Doom, Invasion of the Time Troopers,* and *Lost in Cydonia*). He has collaborated with Pat Williams on more than a dozen books, including *Go for the Magic, Coaching Your Kids to Be Leaders, How to Be Like Jesus* and *How to Be Like Walt Disney.* Jim Denney lives with his wife and two children in California.